Cambridge Latin Course
SECOND EDITION

Unit IIIA

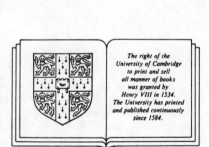

The right of the
University of Cambridge
to print and sell
all manner of books
was granted by
Henry VIII in 1534.
The University has printed
and published continuously
since 1584.

CAMBRIDGE UNIVERSITY PRESS

Cambridge

New York   Port Chester

Melbourne   Sydney

Published by the Press Syndicate of the University of Cambridge
The Pitt Building, Trumpington Street, Cambridge CB2 1RP
40 West 20th Street, New York, NY 10011, USA
10 Stamford Road, Oakleigh, Melbourne 3166, Australia

This book, an outcome of work jointly commissioned by the Schools Council
before its closure and the Cambridge School Classics Project, is published
under the aegis of the School Curriculum Development Committee,
Newcombe House, 45 Notting Hill Gate, London W11 3JB.

First published 1972
Seventh printing 1982
Second edition 1983
Tenth printing 1989

Printed in Great Britain at the
University Press, Cambridge

Library of Congress catalogue card number: 83–10157

ISBN 0 521 28748 0

DS

Thanks are due to the following for permission to reproduce photographs:
pp.11, 21, 35, 57 Bath Museums Services; p.22 photograph by Bob Wilkins, copyright
Bath Archaeological Trust; pp.28, 79 (top) reproduced by courtesy of the Trustees of the
British Museum; p.54 Museo Civico, Piacenza; p.71 Cambridge University Collection,
copyright reserved; p.73 Rheinisches Landesmuseum Trier; p.79 (bottom) The Museum
of London; p.80 Rijksmuseum G.M. Kam; p.92 The Mansell Collection; p.108 (top), 125
The Grosvenor Museum, Chester; p.108 (bottom) copyright Verulamium Museum; p.141
Werner Forman Archive.

Map by Reg Piggott

Drawings by Peter Kesteven, Joy Mellor and Leslie Jones

Contents

Aquae Sūlis

in oppidō Aquīs Sūlis labōrābant multī fabrī, quī thermās maximās exstruēbant. architectus Rōmānus fabrōs īnspiciēbat.

faber prīmus statuam deae Sūlis sculpēbat.

architectus fabrum laudāvit, quod perītus erat et dīligenter labōrābat.

faber, ab architectō laudātus, laetissimus erat.

faber secundus mūrum circum fontem pōnēbat.
architectus fabrum incitāvit, quod fessus erat et lentē labōrābat.
faber, ab architectō incitātus, rem graviter ferēbat. nihil tamen
dīxit, quod architectum timēbat.

faber tertius aquam ad balneum ē fonte sacrō portābat.
architectus fabrum vituperāvit, quod ignāvus erat et minimē
labōrābat.
faber, ab architectō vituperātus, īnsolenter respondit.

3

architectus, ubi verba īnsolentia fabrī audīvit, servōs suōs
arcessīvit.

servī, ab architectō arcessītī, fabrum comprehendērunt et in
balneum dēiēcērunt.

'linguam sordidam habēs', inquit architectus cachinnāns. 'melius
est tibi aquam sacram bibere.'

fōns sacer

Quīntus apud Salvium manēbat per tōtam hiemem. saepe ad aulam Cogidubnī ībat, ā rēge invītātus. Quīntus eī multa dē vītā suā nārrābat, quod rēx aliquid novī audīre semper volēbat.

ubi vēr appropinquābat, Cogidubnus in morbum gravem incidit. multī medicī, ad aulam arcessītī, remedium morbī quaesīvērunt. 5 ingravēscēbat tamen morbus. rēx Quīntum et Salvium dē remediō anxius cōnsuluit.

'mī Quīnte', inquit, 'tū es vir magnae prūdentiae. volō tē mihi cōnsilium dare. ad fontem sacrum īre dēbeō?'

fōns *fountain, spring*
aliquid novī *something new*
morbum: morbus *illness*
gravem: gravis *serious*
cōnsuluit: cōnsulere *consult*
vir magnae prūdentiae *a man of great prudence, a man of good sense*
cōnsilium *advice*

'ubi est iste fōns?' rogāvit Quīntus.   10

'est in oppidō Aquīs Sūlis', respondit Cogidubnus. 'multī aegrōtī,
quī ex hōc fonte aquam bibērunt, posteā convaluērunt. architectum
Rōmānum illūc mīsī, quī thermās maximās exstrūxit. prope
thermās stat templum deae Sūlis, ā meīs fabrīs aedificātum. ego
deam saepe honōrāvī; nunc fortasse dea mē sānāre potest. Salvī, tū 15
es vir magnae calliditātis; volō tē mihi cōnsilium dare. quid facere
dēbeō?'

'tū es vir sapiēns', respondit ille. 'melius est tibi testāmentum
facere.'

oppidō: oppidum *town*
Aquīs Sūlis: Aquae Sūlis *Bath*
aegrōtī: aegrōtus *invalid*
convaluērunt: convalēscere *get better, recover*
exstrūxit: exstruere *build*
calliditātis: calliditās *cleverness, shrewdness*

When you have read section I of this story, answer the questions at the end of the section.

Lūcius Marcius Memor

I

oppidum Aquae Sūlis parvum erat, thermae maximae. prōcūrātor thermārum erat Lūcius Marcius Memor, nōtissimus haruspex, homō obēsus et ignāvus. quamquam iam tertia hōra erat, Memor in cubiculō ēbrius dormiēbat. Cephalus, haruspicis lībertus, Memorem excitāre temptābat.   5

prōcūrātor *manager*
haruspex *soothsayer*
obēsus *fat*

'domine! domine!' clāmābat.

haruspex, graviter dormiēns, nihil respondit.

'dominus nimium vīnī rūrsus bibit', sibi dīxit lībertus. 'domine! surge! hōra tertia est.'

Memor, ā lībertō tandem excitātus, ūnum oculum aperuit. 10

'fer mihi plūs vīnī!' inquit. 'tum abī!'

'domine! domine! necesse est tibi surgere', inquit Cephalus.

'cūr mē vexās, Cephale?' respondit Memor. 'cūr tū rem administrāre ipse nōn potes?'

'rem huius modī administrāre nōn possum', respondit lībertus. 15 'sunt multī servī, multī fabrī, quī mandāta prōcūrātōris exspectant. tē exspectat architectus ipse, vir magnae dignitātis. tē exspectant aegrōtī. adstant sacerdōtēs parātī. adsunt mercātōrēs, quōs arcessīvistī. tū rem ipse administrāre dēbēs.'

'numquam dēsinit labor', clāmāvit Memor. 'quam fessus sum! 20 cūr ad hunc populum barbarum umquam vēnī?'

Cephalus, quī rīsum cēlāre temptābat, Memorī respondit,

'haruspex callidissimus es. nōnne aegrōtīs remedia praebēre vīs? nōnne Britannīs mōrēs Rōmānōs impōnere vīs?'

'es homō magnae stultitiae', respondit Memor. 'aegrōtōs floccī 25 nōn faciō. Britannōs etiam minōris pretiī habeō. sed nunc mihi commodum est hoc tam molestum officium agere. sīc enim ad maiōrēs honōrēs ascendere possum. ego virōs potentēs colere velim. ēheu! in hāc īnsulā sunt paucī virī potentēs, paucī clārī.'

'quid vīs mē facere, Memor?' rogāvit lībertus. 30

'iubeō tē omnēs dīmittere', clāmāvit Memor. 'nōlī mē iterum vexāre!'

Memor, postquam haec verba dīxit, statim obdormīvit. Cephalus, ā dominō īrātō territus, invītus exiit. extrā cubiculum multitūdinem aegrōtōrum invēnit, Memorem exspectantium et 35 vehementer clāmantium. inter aegrōtōs erant nōnnūllī mīlitēs, ab hostibus nūper vulnerātī et paene interfectī. adstābant quoque multī fabrī, Memorem absentem vituperantēs. eōs omnēs Cephalus dīmīsit.

graviter *heavily, soundly*
nimium vīnī *too much wine*
rūrsus *again*
fer! *bring!*
plūs vīnī *more wine*
huius modī *of this kind*
mandāta *instructions, orders*
dignitātis: dignitās *importance, prestige*
adstant: adstāre *stand by*
dēsinit: dēsinere *end, cease*
labor *work*
populum: populus *people*
umquam *ever*
rīsum: rīsus *smile*
praebēre *provide*
mōrēs: mōs *custom*

impōnere *impose*
stultitiae: stultitia *stupidity*
etiam minōris pretiī habeō *I care even
     less about*
officium *duty*
sīc *in this way*
honōrēs: honor *honour*
potentēs: potēns *powerful*
colere *seek favour of, make friends with*
velim *I should like*
clārī: clārus *famous, distinguished*
haec verba *these words*
territus: terrēre *frighten*
hostibus: hostis *enemy*
absentem: absēns *absent*

1 What is the time of day at the start of this story? What is Memor's freedman trying to do?
2 What does the word 'rūrsus' (line 8) suggest about Memor's habits?
3 How many different groups and individuals are waiting to see Memor, according to Cephalus (lines 16–18)?
4 Why does Cephalus say 'mandāta prōcūrātōris' (line 16) rather than 'mandāta tua'?
5 What do you think makes Cephalus smile (line 22)? Why does he try to hide the smile?
6 According to Cephalus (lines 23–4), what were Memor's reasons for coming to work at Bath? Does Cephalus mean this seriously?
7 According to Memor himself (lines 27–8), what was his real reason for coming to Bath? Why has he found it hard to achieve what he wanted?
8 In line 31, Memor says 'iubeō tē omnēs dīmittere'. Which words in the last paragraph tell you that this order was obeyed?

II

mox tamen, Cephalus cubiculum rūrsus intrāvit Memoremque dormientem excitāvit. Memor, simulac Cephalum vīdit, īrātus clāmāvit,

'cūr prohibēs mē dormīre? cūr mihi nōn pārēs? stultior es quam asinus.'   5

'sed domine', respondit Cephalus, 'aliquid novī nūntiāre volō. postquam hinc discessī, mandāta, quae mihi dedistī, effēcī. ubi tamen aegrōtōs fabrōsque dīmittēbam, senātōrem thermīs appropinquantem cōnspexī.'

'quis est ille senātor?' rogāvit Memor, valdē vexātus. 'unde vēnit? 10 senātōrem vidēre nōlō.'

'melius est tibi hunc senātōrem vidēre', respondit Cephalus. 'nam Gāius Salvius est.'

'num Gāius Salvius Līberālis?' exclāmāvit Memor. 'nōn crēdō tibi.'   15

Cephalus tamen facile eī persuāsit, quod Salvius iam in āream thermārum equitābat.

Memor perterritus statim clāmāvit,

'fer mihi togam! fer calceōs! ōrnāmenta mea ubi sunt? vocā servōs! quam īnfēlīx sum! Salvius hūc venit, vir summae 20 auctōritātis, quem colere maximē volō.'

Memor celerrimē togam calceōsque induit. Cephalus eī ōrnāmenta trādidit, ex armāriō raptim extracta. haruspex lībertum innocentem vituperābat, lībertus Salvium.

prohibēs: prohibēre *prevent*
hinc *from here*
effēcī: efficere *carry out, accomplish*
calceōs: calceus *shoe*
ōrnāmenta *decorations*
auctōritātis: auctōritās *authority*
raptim *hastily, quickly*

Base of a statue dedicated to the goddess Sulis by Lucius Marcius Memor

About the language

1   In Stage 20, you met sentences like these, containing *present* participles:

servī per vīllam contendērunt, arāneās **quaerentēs**.
The slaves hurried through the house, looking for spiders' webs.

astrologus, amulētum **tenēns**, ad nōs accurrit.
The astrologer, holding an amulet, ran up to us.

2   In Stage 21, you have met sentences like these:

Memor, ā lībertō **excitātus**, īrātissimus erat.
Memor, having been awakened by the freedman, was very angry.

templum, ā fabrīs perītīs **ōrnātum**, splendidissimum erat.
The temple, having been decorated by skilful craftsmen, was very impressive.

The words in heavy print are *perfect* participles.

3   A perfect participle is used to describe a noun. For instance, in the first example in paragraph 2, 'excitātus' describes Memor.

4   Translate the following examples:

1 servus, ā dominō verberātus, ē vīllā fūgit.
2 saltātrīx, ā spectātōribus laudāta, rīsit.
3 nūntius, ad rēgem arcessītus, rem terribilem nārrāvit.

Pick out the perfect participle in each sentence and find the noun which it describes.

5   A perfect participle changes its ending to agree with the noun it describes. For example:

singular fūr, ā centuriōne superātus, veniam petīvit.
plural   fūrēs, ā centuriōne superātī, veniam petīvērunt.

6 Translate the following examples and pick out the perfect participle in each sentence:

1 senex, ab astrologō monitus, nāvigāre nōluit.
2 prīncipēs, ā rēge vocātī, celeriter ad aulam vēnērunt.
3 cēna, ā coquō Graecō parāta, omnēs hospitēs dēlectāvit.

Find the noun which each perfect participle is describing and say whether each noun-and-participle pair is singular or plural.

7 There are two kinds of perfect participle in Latin. The one described in this Stage is known as the *perfect passive* participle. You will meet the other kind in Stage 22.

8 Notice two different ways of translating perfect passive participles:

architectus, ā Cogidubnō ipsō missus, thermās maximās exstrūxit.
The architect, having been sent by Cogidubnus himself, built some very large baths.
   or, in more natural English,
The architect, sent by Cogidubnus himself, built some very large baths.

mercātōrēs, ā latrōnibus graviter vulnerātī, in fossā iacēbant.
The merchants, having been seriously wounded by robbers, were lying in the ditch.
The merchants, seriously wounded by robbers, were lying in the ditch.

Memor rem suscipit

Salvius et Memor, in hortō sōlī ambulantēs, sermōnem gravem habent.

Salvius: Lūcī Marcī Memor, vir summae prūdentiae es. volō tē
rem magnam suscipere.

Memor: tālem rem suscipere velim, sed occupātissimus sum.
exspectant mē aegrōtī et sacerdōtēs. vexant mē 5
architectus et fabrī. sed quid vīs mē facere?

Salvius: Tiberius Claudius Cogidubnus, rēx Rēgnēnsium, hūc
nūper advēnit. Cogidubnus, quī in morbum gravem
incidit, aquam ē fonte sacrō bibere vult.

Memor: difficile est mihi tē adiuvāre, mī senātor. Cogidubnus est 10
vir octōgintā annōrum. difficile est deae Sūlī Cogidubnum sānāre.

Salvius: nōlō tē reddere Cogidubnum sānum. volō tē rem
contrāriam efficere.

Memor: quid dīcis? num mortem Cogidubnī cupis? 15

Salvius: ita vērō! porrō, quamquam tam occupātus es, volō tē
ipsum hanc rem efficere.

Memor: vīsne mē mortem eī parāre? rem huius modī facere nōn
ausim. Cogidubnus enim est vir clārissimus, ā populō
Rōmānō honōrātus. 20

Salvius: es vir summae calliditātis. hanc rem efficere potes. nōn
sōlum ego, sed etiam Imperātor, hoc cupit. Cogidubnus
enim Rōmānōs saepe vexāvit. Imperātor mihi, nōn
Cogidubnō, cōnfīdit. Imperātor tibi praemium dignum
prōmittit. num praemium recūsāre vīs, tibi ab 25
Imperātōre prōmissum?

Memor: quō modō id facere possum?

Salvius: nescio. hoc tantum tibi dīcō: Imperātor mortem
Cogidubnī exspectat.

Memor: ō mē miserum! rem difficiliōrem numquam fēcī. 30

Salvius: vīta, mī Memor, est plēna rērum difficilium.
(*exit Salvius.*)

Memor: Cephale! Cephale! (*lībertus, ā Memore vocātus, celeriter
            intrat. pōculum vīnī fert.*) cūr mihi vīnum offers? nōn
            vīnum, sed cōnsilium quaerō. iubeō tē mihi cōnsilium 35
            quam celerrimē dare. rēx Cogidubnus hūc vēnit,
            remedium morbī petēns. Imperātor, ā Cogidubnō saepe
            vexātus, iam mortem eius cupit. Imperātor ipse iubet
            mē hoc efficere. quam difficile est!

Cephalus: minimē, facile est! pōculum venēnātum habeō, mihi ā 40
            latrōne Aegyptiō ōlim datum. venēnum, in pōculō
            cēlātum, vītam celerrimē exstinguere potest.

Memor: cōnsilium, quod mihi prōpōnis, perīculōsum est.
            Cogidubnō venēnum dare timeō.

Cephalus: nihil perīculī est. rēx, quotiēns ē balneō exiit, ad fontem 45
            deae īre solet. tum necesse est servō prope fontem deae
            stāre et pōculum rēgī offerre.

Memor: (*dēlectātus*) cōnsilium optimum est. nūllīs tamen servīs
            cōnfīdere ausim. sed tibi cōnfīdō, Cephale. iubeō tē
            ipsum Cogidubnō pōculum offerre.   50

Cephalus: ēheu! vīta lībertī dūra est. mihi rem difficillimam
            impōnis.

Memor: vīta, mī Cephale, est plēna rērum difficilium.

tālem: tālis *such*	nescio: nescīre *not know*
octōgintā *eighty*	venēnātum: venēnātus *poisoned*
reddere *make*	datum: dare *give*
sānum: sānus *well, healthy*	venēnum *poison*
rem contrāriam: rēs contrāria	exstinguere *extinguish, destroy*
the opposite	prōpōnis: prōpōnere *propose, put forward*
porrō *what's more, furthermore*	nihil perīculī *no danger*
nōn ausim *I shouldn't dare*	quotiēns *whenever*
nōn sōlum . . . sed etiam *not only*	balneō: balneum *bath*
. . . *but also*	difficillimam: difficillimus *very difficult*
dignum: dignus *worthy, appropriate*	

About the language

1   Study the following examples:

> plūs cibī   more food
> nimium vīnī   too much wine

Each example is made up of two words:

1 a word like 'plūs' or 'nimium' which indicates an *amount* or *quantity*,
2 a noun in the *genitive* case.

2   Further examples:

> satis pecūniae   nimium perīculī
> nimium cibī   plūs sanguinis
> plūs labōris   satis aquae

Practising the language

1   Study the form and meaning of the following words, and give the meaning of the untranslated ones:

laetus	happy	laetē	happily
perītus	skilful	perītē	skilfully
stultissimus	very foolish	stultissimē	very foolishly
tacitus	silent	tacitē	
cautus	cautious	cautē	
probus		probē	honestly
callidus		callidē	cleverly, cunningly
superbus	proud	superbē	
crūdēlissimus	very cruel	crūdēlissimē	
sevērissimus	very severe	sevērissimē	
līberālissimus		līberālissimē	very generously

The words in the left-hand pair of columns are *adjectives*. Adjectives were described in Stage 14 and the Language Information pamphlets of Units IIA and IIB.

The words in the right-hand pair of columns are known as *adverbs*.

Give the meaning of the following adverbs:

intentē, firmē, stultē, saevē, dīligentissimē

2 Complete each sentence with the right word and then translate.

1 omnēs aegrōtī . . . . . vīsitāre volēbant. (fōns, fontem, fontis)
2 plūrimī servī in fundō . . . . . labōrābant. (dominus, dominum, dominī)
3 'fortasse . . . . . morbum meum sānāre potest', inquit rēx. (dea, deam, deae)
4 . . . . . Cogidubnum laudāvērunt, quod līberālis et sapiēns erat. (prīncipēs, prīncipum)
5 mercātor, postquam . . . . . in saccō posuit, ē forō discessit. (dēnāriī, dēnāriōs, dēnāriōrum)
6 senex, quī in Arabiā diū habitāverat, magnum numerum . . . . . collēgerat. (gemmae, gemmās, gemmārum)

3 Complete each sentence with the right word from the list below and then translate.

parāvī, rapuērunt, amīcōrum, hastam, nūntius, hospitibus

1 puer, in cubiculō dormiēns, vōcēs . . . . . nōn audīvit.
2 'optimam cēnam tibi . . . . ., domine', inquit coquus.
3 senex, quī avārus erat, ... vīnum offerre nōlēbat.
4 in rīpā flūminis stābat servus, quī . . . . . in manibus tenēbat.
5 subitō latrōnēs irrūpērunt et pecūniam . . . . . .
6 . . . . ., quem rēx mīserat, epistulam in itinere āmīsit.

4 Translate each English sentence into Latin by selecting correctly from the pairs of Latin words.

For example: The messenger heard the voice of the old man.

> nūntius vōcem senem audīvī
> nūntium vōcī senis audīvit

Answer: nūntius vōcem senis audīvit.

1 The priests showed the statue to the architect.

> sacerdōtēs statuam architectum ostendit
> sacerdōtibus statuās architectō ostendērunt

2 The king praised the skilful doctor.

> rēx medicus perītum laudāvit
> rēgēs medicum perītī laudāvērunt

3 A friend of the soldiers was visiting the temple.

> amīcus mīlitis templum vīsitābat
> amīcō mīlitum templī vīsitāvit

4 The shouts of the invalids had annoyed the soothsayer.

> clāmōrem aegrōtī haruspicem vexāverant
> clāmōrēs aegrōtōrum haruspicēs vexāvērunt

5 We handed over the master's money to the farmers.

> pecūnia dominum agricolās trādidimus
> pecūniam dominī agricolīs trādidērunt

5 Complete each sentence with the right word and then translate.

1 tū ipse hanc rem administrāre . . . . . .(dēbeō, dēbēs, dēbet)

2 'domine! surge!' clāmāvit Cephalus. 'nam Gāius Salvius thermīs . . . . . .' (appropinquō, appropinquās, appropinquat)

3 cūr mē vituperās? herī per tōtum diem . . . . (labōrāvī, labōrāvistī, labōrāvit)

4 ego, quod fontem sacrum vidēre . . . . . ., iter ad oppidum Aquās Sūlis fēcī. (cupiēbam, cupiēbās, cupiēbat)

5 lībertus, quī senātōrem . . . . ., in cubiculum haruspicis ruit. (cōnspexeram, cōnspexerās, cōnspexerat)

6 ubi poēta versum scurrīlem recitāvit, amīcus meus īrātus erat; ego tamen . . . . . . (rīsī, rīsistī, rīsit)

7 ē lectō surrēxī, quod dormīre nōn . . . . . . (poteram, poterās, poterat)

8 in hāc vīllā . . . . . Memor, haruspex nōtissimus. (habitō, habitās, habitat)

Aquae Sulis and its baths

The modern city of Bath lies in the valley of the river Avon, just to the east of Bristol. In a small area of low-lying ground, enclosed by a bend in the river, mineral springs of hot water emerge from underground at the rate of over a million litres (a quarter of a million gallons) a day. The water has a temperature of between 40 and 49 degrees centigrade (104 and 121 degrees fahrenheit). It has a low mineral content (calcium, magnesium and sodium are the main minerals) and microscopic traces of radium. It was here that the Celts who lived in the surrounding hills came to worship the goddess of the spring, Sulis, long before the Romans arrived in Britain. The Celts clearly recognised the power of the goddess to produce hot water from the ground, but they also saw the power of the goddess in the healing properties of the spring water.

As Roman settlers moved gradually westwards after the invasion of A.D. 43, they soon brought changes to the region. Much of the rich farmland owned by Celtic farmers was taken over and turned into villa estates in the Roman style. The Romans recognised that the springs of Sulis were an important religious centre and they erected huge public baths and other buildings so that visitors might enjoy the healing properties of the hot mineral waters in comfort. No doubt the heat helped relieve conditions such as rheumatism and arthritis, but many people must have visited the baths in the hope of miraculous cures for all kinds of diseases. During the latter part of the first century A.D. the new Romano-British town of Aquae Sulis began to grow up. The Roman writer, Pliny the Elder, said in his *Natural History*: 'Healing springs help to encourage the growth of towns' and Aquae Sulis was no exception. The healing springs, a mild climate and a sheltered position were all reasons why the town developed as an important spa.

The Roman masons had good supplies of limestone quarried locally, and the nearby Mendip Hills provided the lead needed for lining the baths. The main building was a long, rectangular structure, larger and more magnificent than any other set of baths west of Rome at this date. It contained three main plunge baths filled with a constant supply of water at a pleasant temperature. The water was brought from the hot spring through lead pipes. The pool nearest the spring naturally contained the hottest water, whereas the furthest pool was the coolest, since the water lost much of its heat on the way to it. To provide a focal point for visitors to the baths, the Romans surrounded the spring with a lead-lined reservoir some 12–15 metres (40–50 feet) across. At a later date, they built a viewing platform and roofed the entire structure.

Temple and baths at Aquae Sulis (1st century A.D.)

Aquae Sulis lay within tribal territory over which Cogidubnus may have had control. It is just possible that he himself was responsible for or at least had a hand in the development of the town. This building project certainly matched the splendour of the palace at Fishbourne which was erected at about the same time.

At the time of our story (A.D. 83), Aquae Sulis was a small but growing community. The bath buildings were still being erected but were already the most impressive feature of the town. There were probably a few other public buildings, such as a 'basilica' (hall) for the administration of law and local government, and possibly a theatre, but most of the other buildings would have been houses for those who had already made their home in the town, and inns for the town's many visitors.

Some people travelled long distances to Aquae Sulis, attracted by the fame of its spring and hoping that the healing power of the waters would cure their illnesses. One elderly woman, Rusonia Aventina, came from Metz in eastern Gaul. Her tombstone shows that she died at Aquae Sulis at the age of fifty-eight, perhaps from the illness which she had hoped the spring would cure. Julius Vitalis was a soldier serving as armourer to the Twentieth Legion, based at Chester. His tombstone shows that he had served for just nine years

The Great Bath

when he died at the age of twenty-nine; possibly his commanding officer had sent him to Aquae Sulis on sick leave. But many visitors came and departed in good health.

The Roman authorities were quick to realise that Aquae Sulis was becoming a popular place of pilgrimage. Visitors entering the new bath buildings and seeing the mysterious hot waters bubbling in the newly built reservoir would feel that they were entering a holy place. They thought that a cure for their ailments depended as much on divine favour as on the medicinal powers of the water. A temple was therefore constructed next to the bath buildings and dedicated to the goddess Sulis Minerva. By linking the two names in this way, the Romans encouraged the British people to worship Minerva, goddess of healing and the arts, together with their own goddess, Sulis. The temple stood in a specially enclosed area, with a

Inscribed pewter and silver bowls thrown as offerings into the sacred spring

magnificent altar in front and a bronze statue of the goddess inside.

The appointment of a Roman official, Lucius Marcius Memor, to take charge of the religious activities at Aquae Sulis is another example of the Romans' efforts to spread Roman ways and customs among the Britons. In the story on page 8 he complains of having to live and work in Britain, but he reluctantly accepts that this is necessary if he is to further his career back in Rome. Clearly, Memor has been posted to the province of Britain to help promote the Roman way of life. Many such officials must have contributed to the policy of 'romanisation' in this way.

Aquae Sulis was, of course, something of a tourist centre as well as a place of religious pilgrimage, and one can imagine the entrance to the baths crowded with souvenir stalls and sellers of lucky charms. Visitors would often buy such offerings to throw into the sacred spring with a prayer for future good health. These offerings were sometimes expensive: they included, for example, beautifully carved gemstones and other items of jewellery.

The full extent of the bath and temple buildings is only gradually becoming known to us from the work of archaeologists. The most recent excavations have revealed the details of construction of the Roman reservoir surrounding the hot spring itself, and important work was carried out in 1982 on the temple precinct. The results of these excavations are on display in the museum. Many thousands of Roman coins have been recovered from the spring, together with silver and pewter vessels thrown in as offerings to the goddess. About fifty small sheets of lead or pewter were also found with Latin inscriptions on them. Their translations show that some people were anxious to use the powers of Sulis Minerva for more sinister purposes than good health, as we shall see in Stage 22.

Words and phrases checklist

From now on, most verbs in the checklists are listed as in the Unit IIIA Language Information pamphlet (i.e. perfect passive participles are usually included).

ā, ab – by
adiuvō, adiuvāre, adiūvī – help
annus, annī – year
ascendō, ascendere, ascendī – climb, rise
barbarus, barbarī – barbarian
cēlō, cēlāre, cēlāvī, cēlātus – hide
circum – around
cōnfīdō, cōnfīdere – trust
dēiciō, dēicere, dēiēcī, dēiectus – throw down
dūrus, dūra, dūrum – harsh, hard
efficiō, efficere, effēcī, effectus – carry out, accomplish
extrahō, extrahere, extrāxī, extractus – drag out, pull out
fōns, fontis – fountain, spring
gravis, grave – heavy, serious
haruspex, haruspicis – soothsayer
hōra, hōrae – hour
īnfēlīx, *gen.* īnfēlīcis – unlucky
iubeō, iubēre, iussī, iussus – order
morbus, morbī – illness
nōnnūllī, nōnnūllae – some, several
nūper – recently
occupātus, occupāta, occupātum – busy
oppidum, oppidī – town
perītus, perīta, perītum – skilful
plēnus, plēna, plēnum – full
plūs, *gen.* plūris – more
pretium, pretiī – price
sapiēns, *gen.* sapientis – wise
suscipiō, suscipere, suscēpī, susceptus – undertake, take on
unde – from where

dēfīxiō

fūr thermīs cautē
appropinquāvit.
fūr, thermās ingressus, ad
fontem sacrum festīnāvit.

fūr, prope fontem stāns,
circumspectāvit.
fūr, senem cōnspicātus, post
columnam sē cēlāvit.

senex, amulētum aureum tenēns,
ad fontem prōcessit.
senex oculōs ad caelum sustulit
et deae Sūlī precēs adhibuit.

senex, deam precātus, amulētum
in fontem iniēcit et exiit.

fūr, quī amulētum aureum
vīderat, ad fontem iterum
festīnāvit.
fūr, ad fontem regressus,
amulētum in aquā quaesīvit.

fūr, amulētum adeptus, attonitus lēgit:

MORTEM OMNIBVS FVRIBVS

fūr amulētum dēiēcit et ē thermīs perterritus fūgit.

Vilbia

Vilbia et Rubria, pōcula sordida lavantēs, in culīnā tabernae garriēbant. hae puellae erant fīliae Latrōnis. Latrō, quī tabernam tenēbat, erat vir magnae dīligentiae sed minimae prūdentiae. Latrō, culīnam ingressus, puellās castīgābat.

'multa sunt pōcula sordida. iubeō vōs pōcula quam celerrimē 5 lavāre. labōrāte! nōlīte garrīre! loquāciōrēs estis quam psittacī.'

Latrō, haec verba locūtus, exiit.

Vilbia, tamen, quae pulchra et obstināta erat, patrem floccī nōn faciēbat. pōcula nōn lāvit, sed Rubriae fībulam ostendit. Rubria fībulam, quam soror tenēbat, avidē spectāvit.   10

Rubria: quam pulchra, quam pretiōsa est haec fībula, mea Vilbia! eam īnspicere velim. quis tibi dedit? num argentea est?

Vilbia: sānē argentea est. Modestus, mīles Rōmānus, eam mihi dedit.

Rubria: quālis est hic mīles? estne homō mendāx, sīcut cēterī 15 mīlitēs Rōmānī? multī mīlitēs vulnera ´fingunt, quod perīcula bellī vītāre volunt. Modestus quoque ignāvus est?

Vilbia: minimē! est vir maximae virtūtis. ōlim tria mīlia hostium occīdit. nunc lēgātum ipsum custōdit.

Rubria: Herculēs alter est! ego autem tālēs fābulās saepe ex aliīs 20 mīlitibus audīvī.

Vilbia: cēterī mīlitēs mendācēs sunt, Modestus probus. Modestus hūc vēnit aeger. Modestus, in thermās ingressus, aquam sacram bibit. Modestus, deam Sūlem precātus, statim convaluit.   2

Rubria: dissentīre nōn ausim. quō modō huic tam mīrābilī mīlitī occurristī?

Vilbia: simulac tabernam nostram intrāvit Modestus, eum statim amāvī. quantī erant lacertī eius! quanta bracchia!

Rubria: tibi favet fortūna, mea Vilbia. quid autem dē Bulbō dīcis, quem ōlim amābās? tibi perīculōsum est Bulbum contemnere, quod rēs magicās intellegit.

Vilbia: nōlī illam pestem commemorāre! Bulbus, saepe dē mātrimōniō locūtus, nihil umquam effēcit. sed Modestus, quī fortissimus et audācissimus est, mē cūrāre potest. 35 Modestus nunc est suspīrium meum.

dīligentiae: dīligentia *industry, hard work*
minimae: minimus *very little*
ingressus *having entered*
locūtus *having spoken*
fībulam: fībula *brooch*
avidē *eagerly*
quālis? *what sort of man?*
vulnera fingunt *pretend to be wounded, invent wounds*
bellī: bellum *war*
virtūtis: virtūs *courage*
tria mīlia *three thousand*
occīdit: occīdere *kill*
lēgātum: lēgātus *commander*
alter *another, a second*
autem *but*
precātus *having prayed to*
huic *this (dative of* hic)
occurristī: occurrere *meet*
quantī: quantus *how big*
lacertī: lacertus *muscle*
bracchia *arms*
contemnere *reject, despise*
mātrimōniō: mātrimōnium *marriage*
suspīrium *heart-throb*

Modestus

Modestus et Strȳthiō ad tabernam Latrōnis ambulant. Strȳthiō, quamquam amīcus Modestū est, eum dērīdet.

Modestus: ubi es, Strȳthiō? iubeō tē prope mē stāre.

Strȳthiō: adsum. hercle! quam fortūnātus sum! prope virum summae virtūtis sum. tū enim fortior es quam Mārs ipse. 5

Modestus: vērum dīcis. ōlim tria mīlia hostium occīdī.

Strȳthiō: tē omnēs puellae amant, quod tam fortis et pulcher es. illa Vilbia, heri tē cōnspicāta, statim amāvit. multa dē tē rogāvit. 10

Modestus: quid dīxit?

Strȳthiō: mē avidē rogāvit, 'estne Herculēs?' 'minimē! est frāter eius', respondī. tum fībulam, quam puella alia tibi dederat, Vilbiae trādidī. 'Modestus, vir benignus et nōbilis', inquam, 'tibi hanc fībulam grātīs dat.' Vilbia, 15 fībulam adepta, mihi respondit, 'quam pulcher Modestus est! quam līberālis! velim cum eō colloquium habēre.'

Modestus: ēheu! nōnne molestae sunt puellae? mihi difficile est puellās vītāre. nimis pulcher sum. 20

Strȳthiō: ecce! ad tabernam Latrōnis advēnimus. fortasse inest Vilbia, quae tē tamquam deum adōrat.
(tabernam intrant.)

Mārs *Mars (god of war)*
vērum *the truth*
cōnspicāta: cōnspicātus *having caught sight of*
inquam *I said*
grātīs *free*
adepta: adeptus *having received, having obtained*
colloquium *talk, chat*
nimis *too*
inest: inesse *be inside*
tamquam *as, like*

About the language

1 In Stage 21 you met sentences containing *perfect passive* participles:

rēx, ā Rōmānīs **honōrātus**, semper fidēlis manēbat.
The king, having been honoured by the Romans, always remained loyal.

puerī, ā custōde **monitī**, ad vīllam rediērunt.
The boys, having been warned by the guard, returned to the house.

2 In Stage 22, you have met another kind of perfect participle. Study the way it is translated in the following examples:

Vilbia, culīnam **ingressa**, sorōrī fībulam ostendit.
Vilbia, having entered the kitchen, showed the brooch to her sister.

senex, haec verba **locūtus**, abiit.
The old man, having said these words, went away.

This kind of participle is a *perfect active* participle.

3 Translate the following examples and pick out the perfect active participle in each sentence:

1 iuvenis, ad thermās regressus, amīcum quaesīvit.
2 puellae, leōnem cōnspicātae, ad vīllam statim ruērunt.
3 mercātōrēs, pecūniam adeptī, ad nāvēs contendērunt.
4 ancilla, deam precāta, ā templō discessit.

Find the noun which each participle is describing.

amor omnia vincit

scaena prīma

Bulbus et amīcus in tabernā Latrōnis sunt. vīnum bibunt āleamque lūdunt.
Bulbus amīcō multam pecūniam dēbet.

Gutta (*amīcus Bulbī*): quam īnfēlīx es! nōn sōlum puellam, sed etiam
      pecūniam āmīsistī.

Bulbus: pecūniam floccī nōn faciō, sed puellam, quam maximē 5
      amō, āmittere nōlō.

Gutta: quō modō eam retinēre potes? mīles Rōmānus, vir summae
      virtūtis, eam petit. heus! Venerem iactāvī! caupō! iubeō tē
      plūs vīnī ferre.

Bulbus: mīles, quī eam dēcēpit, homō mendāx, prāvus, ignāvus est. 10
      Vilbia, ab eō dēcepta, nunc mē contemnit. eam saepe
      monuī, 'nōlī mīlitibus crēdere, praesertim Rōmānīs.'
      Vilbia tamen, hunc Modestum cōnspicāta, statim eum
      amāvit.

Gutta: puellīs nōn tūtum est per viās huius oppidī īre. tanta est 15
      arrogantia hōrum mīlitum. hercle! tū etiam īnfēlīcior es.
      canem iterum iactāvistī. alium dēnārium mihi dēbēs.

Bulbus: dēnārium libenter trādō, nōn puellam. ōdī istum mīlitem.
Modestus tamen puellam retinēre nōn potest, quod
auxilium ā deā petīvī. thermās ingressus, tabulam in 20
fontem sacrum iniēcī. dīra imprecātiō, in tabulā scrīpta,
iam in fonte deae iacet. (*intrant Modestus et Strȳthiō.*) exitium
Modestī laetus exspectō. nihil mihi obstāre potest.
Gutta: hercle! īnfēlīcissimus es. ecce! nōbīs appropinquat ipse
Modestus. necesse est mihi quam celerrimē exīre. 25
(*exit currēns.*)

amor *love*
omnia *all, everything*
scaena *scene*
āleam . . . lūdunt *are playing dice*
Venerem: Venus *Venus (highest throw at dice)*
iactāvī: iactāre *throw*
praesertim *especially*
arrogantia *cheek, arrogance*
canem: canis *dog (lowest throw at dice)*
ōdī *I hate*
tabulam: tabula *tablet, writing-tablet*
imprecātiō *curse*
scrīpta: scrībere *write*
exitium *ruin, destruction*

scaena secunda

Modestus īrātus Bulbum vituperat, quod verba eius audīvit.

Modestus: quid dīcēbās, homuncule? exitium meum exspectās?
asine! tū, quod mīlitem Rōmānum vituperāvistī, in
magnō perīculō es. mihi facile est tē, tamquam hostem,
dīlaniāre. Strȳthiō! tē iubeō hanc pestem verberāre. 5
postquam eum verberāvistī, ē tabernā ēice!

*Strȳthiō invītus Bulbum verberāre incipit. Bulbus, fortiter sē dēfendēns, vīnum
in caput Strȳthiōnis fundit. Modestus Bulbum, simulac tergum vertit, ferōciter
pulsat. Bulbus exanimātus prōcumbit. Vilbia, quae clāmōrēs audīvit, intrat.
ingressa, Bulbum humī iacentem videt et Modestum mollīre incipit.* 10

Vilbia: dēsine, mī Modeste. iste Bulbus, ā tē verberātus, iterum
mē vexāre nōn potest. tū es leō, iste rīdiculus mūs. volō
tē clēmentem esse et Bulbō parcere. placetne tibi?

Modestus: mihi placet. victōribus decōrum est victīs parcere. tē,
nōn istum, quaerō. 15

Vilbia: ō Modeste, quam laeta sum! cūr mē ex omnibus puellīs
ēlēgistī?

Modestus: necesse est nōbīs in locō sēcrētō noctū convenīre.

Vilbia: id facere nōn ausim. pater mē sōlam exīre nōn vult. ubi
est hic locus? 20

Modestus: prope fontem deae Sūlis. nōnne tibi persuādēre
possum?

Vilbia: mihi difficile est iussa patris neglegere, sed tibi resistere
nōn possum.

Modestus: dā mihi ōsculum. 25

Vilbia: ēheu! ō suspīrium meum! mihi necesse est ad culīnam
redīre, tibi noctem exspectāre.

*exeunt. Bulbus, quī magnam partem huius colloquiī audīvit, surgit. quam
celerrimē ēgressus, Guttam petit, cui cōnsilium callidum prōpōnit.*

dīlaniāre *tear to pieces*	sēcrētō: sēcrētus *secret*
ēice: ēicere *throw out*	noctū *by night*
humī *on the ground*	iussa *orders, instructions*
mollīre *soothe*	neglegere *neglect*
clēmentem: clēmēns *merciful*	ēgressus *having gone out*
parcere *spare*	cui *to whom (dative of* quī*)*
victīs: victī *the conquered*	

The sacred spring as it is today

scaena tertia

per silentium noctis thermās intrant Bulbus et Gutta. prope fontem sacrum sē
cēlant. Bulbus Guttae stolam et pallium, quod sēcum tulit, ostendit.

Bulbus: Gutta, volō tē haec vestīmenta induere. volō tē
                persōnam Vilbiae agere. nōbīs necesse est dēcipere
                Modestum, quem brevī exspectō.   5

Gutta: vah! virō nōn decōrum est stolam gerere. praetereā
                barbam habeō.

Bulbus: id minimī mōmentī est, quod in tenebrīs sumus. nōnne
                tibi persuādēre possum? ecce! decem dēnāriōs tibi dō.
                nunc tacē! indue stolam palliumque! stā prope fontem 10
                deae! ubi Modestus fontī appropinquat, dīc eī verba
                suāvissima!

pallium *cloak*	vah! *ugh!*
vestīmenta *clothes*	praetereā *besides*
persōnam Vilbiae agere *play the part of Vilbia*	mōmentī: mōmentum *importance*
brevī *in a short time*	tenebrīs: tenebrae *darkness*

Gutta, postquam stolam invītus induit, prope fontem stat. Modestus, sōlus thermās ingressus, fontī appropinquat.

Modestus: Vilbia, mea Vilbia! Modestus, fortissimus mīlitum, 15
        adest.

Gutta: ō dēliciae meae! venī ad mē.

Modestus: quam rauca est vōx tua! num lacrimās, quod tardus
        adveniō?

Gutta: ita vērō! tam sollicita eram. 20

Modestus: lacrimās tuās siccāre possum. (*Modestus ad Guttam
        advenit.*) dī immortālēs! Vilbia! barbam habēs? quid tibi
        accidit? ō!

*tum Bulbus Modestum in fontem dēicit. Vilbia, thermās ingressa, ubi clāmōrēs
audīvit, prope iānuam perterrita manet.* 25

Modestus: pereō! pereō! parce! parce!

Bulbus: furcifer! Vilbiam meam, quam valdē amō, auferre
        audēs? nunc mihi facile est tē interficere.

Modestus: reddō tibi Vilbiam. nōn amō Vilbiam. eam ā tē auferre
        nōn ausim. nōlī mē innocentem interficere. Vilbiam 30
        floccī nōn faciō.

*Vilbia, simulatque haec audīvit, īrāta fontī appropinquat. Modestum
vituperāre incipit.*

Vilbia: mē floccī nōn facis? ō hominem ignāvum! ego ipsa tē
        dīlaniāre velim. 35

Bulbus: mea Vilbia, victōribus decōrum est victīs parcere.

Vilbia: mī Bulbe, dēliciae meae, miserrima sum! longē errāvī.

Bulbus: nōlī lacrimāre! ego tē cūrāre possum.

Vilbia: ō Bulbe! ō suspīrium meum!

*Bulbus et Vilbia domum redeunt. Gutta stolam palliumque exuit. dēnāriōs laetē
numerat. Modestus ē fonte sē extrahit et madidus abit.*

siccāre *dry*
auferre *take away, steal*
longē errāvī: longē errāre *make a big mistake*
exuit: exuere *take off*

About the language

1 Study the following examples:

homō ingeniī prāvī	a man of evil character
fēmina magnae dignitātis	a woman of great prestige

In each example, a word like 'homō' or 'fēmina' is described by a noun and adjective in the *genitive* case.

2 Notice the different ways of translating such phrases:

puella magnae prūdentiae   a girl of great sense
                                   or, in more natural English:
                           a very sensible girl

vir summae virtūtis   a man of the utmost courage
                                   or, in more natural English:
                           a very courageous man, *or*
                           a very brave man

3 Further examples:

vir magnae auctōritātis	fābula huius modī
homō minimae prūdentiae	iuvenis ingeniī optimī
vir octōgintā annōrum	puella maximae calliditātis

Practising the language

1 Study the form and meaning of the following adjectives and adverbs, and give the meaning of the untranslated words:

brevis	short	breviter	shortly
ferōx	fierce	ferōciter	fiercely
cōmis	polite	cōmiter	
levis		leviter	lightly, slightly
suāvis	sweet	suāviter	
celer		celeriter	quickly
crūdēlis	cruel	crūdēliter	
mollis	soft, gentle	molliter	
pār		pariter	equally
dīligēns	careful	dīligenter	
neglegēns		neglegenter	carelessly
prūdēns	shrewd, sensible	prūdenter	
audāx	bold	audācter	

Give the meaning of the following adverbs:

fidēliter, fortiter, līberāliter, sapienter, īnsolenter

2 Complete each sentence with the right word and then translate.

1 Modestus per viās . . . . . ambulābat, puellās quaerēns. (oppidī, oppidō)
2 Gutta, vir benignus, auxilium . . . . . saepe dabat. (amīcī, amīcō)
3 Rubria, quae in tabernā labōrābat, ... vīnum obtulit. (iuvenis, iuvenī)
4 in vīllā . . . . ., turba ingēns conveniēbat. (haruspicis, haruspicī)
5 tabernārius . . . . . multās rēs pretiōsās ostendit. (ancillārum, ancillīs)
6 dea Sūlis precēs . . . . . audīre solēbat. (aegrōtōrum, aegrōtīs)
7 centuriō gladiōs hastāsque . . . . . īnspicere coepit. (mīlitum, mīlitibus)
8 caupō pessimum vīnum . . . . . praebēbat. (hospitum, hospitibus)

3 Make up six Latin sentences using some of the words in the lists
below. Some of your sentences should contain four words, but
others may contain only three, or two. Write out each sentence
and then translate it.

For example: puer senī pōculum trādidit.
The boy handed the cup to the old man.

cīvēs agricolam salūtāvērunt.
The citizens greeted the farmer.

nautās vīdit.
He saw the sailors.

nominatives	*accusatives*	*datives*	*verbs*
servus	pecūniam	ancillīs	vīdit
servī	equōs	fabrō	vīdērunt
gladiātor	dominum	iuvenibus	trādidit
gladiātōrēs	nautās	centuriōnī	trādidērunt
cīvis	leōnem	hominibus	interfēcit
cīvēs	gemmās	senī	interfēcērunt
fēmina	agricolam	spectātōribus	obtulit
fēminae	librōs	medicō	obtulērunt
puer	mīlitem	amīcīs	salūtāvit
puerī	pōculum	rēgī	salūtāvērunt

Magic and curses

When Roman religious sites are excavated, archaeologists sometimes find lead or pewter tablets inscribed with curses. These are known as 'dēfīxiōnēs'. Many Romans believed it was possible to put a curse on a personal enemy by dedicating him or her to the gods in this way.

Many defixiones have been found in Britain. They include, for example, a defixio placed by a man on a gang that had beaten him up. In another one, a woman curses someone who has falsely accused her of poisoning her husband. Many are directed at thieves.

The method of putting a defixio on somebody was as follows. The name of the offender was written on a small tablet together with details of the crime and the hoped-for punishment. The tablet was then fastened to a tomb with a long nail, or thrown into a well or a spring. To increase the mystery the name was often written backwards and apparently meaningless magical words, such as BESCU, BEREBESCU, BAZAGRA, were also added for effect. Sometimes we find a figure roughly drawn on the tablet, as in the illustration opposite. It depicts a bearded demon, carrying an urn and a torch, which were symbols of death. The boat in which he stands may represent the boat of Charon, the ferryman of the Underworld, who took the souls of the dead across the river Styx.

The wording of the curse can be very simple, just 'I dedicate' followed by the intended victim's name. But sometimes it can be ferociously eloquent, as in the following example: 'May burning fever seize all her limbs, kill her soul and her heart. O Gods of the Underworld, break and smash her bones, choke her, let her body be twisted and shattered – phrix, phrox.'

It may seem strange that religion should be used to bring harm to people in this very direct and spiteful way, but the Romans tended to see their gods as possible allies in the struggles of life. When they wished to injure an enemy, they thought it natural and proper to seek the gods' powerful help.

Words and phrases checklist

adeptus, adepta, adeptum – having received, having obtained

amor, amōris – love

aureus, aurea, aureum – golden, made of gold

avidē – eagerly

caelum, caelī – sky

dēcipiō, dēcipere, dēcēpī, dēceptus – deceive, trick

dīrus, dīra, dīrum – dreadful

dissentiō, dissentīre, dissēnsī – disagree

ēligō, ēligere, ēlēgī, ēlēctus – choose

exitium, exitiī – ruin, destruction

fundō, fundere, fūdī, fūsus – pour

hostis, hostis – enemy

iactō, iactāre, iactāvī, iactātus – throw

incipiō, incipere, incēpī, inceptus – begin

ingressus, ingressa, ingressum – having entered

iniciō, inicere, iniēcī, iniectus – throw in

lacrima, lacrimae – tear

minimus, minima, minimum – very little, least

molestus, molesta, molestum – troublesome

moneō, monēre, monuī, monitus – warn, advise

parcō, parcere, pepercī – spare

precātus, precāta, precātum – having prayed (to)

prūdentia, prūdentiae – prudence, good sense

quantus, quanta, quantum – how big

quō modō? – how?

tardus, tarda, tardum – late

tūtus, tūta, tūtum – safe

verbum, verbī – word

virtūs, virtūtis – courage

vītō, vītāre, vītāvī, vītātus – avoid

haruspex

in thermīs

I

prope thermās erat templum, ā fabrīs Cogidubnī aedificātum. in
hōc templō aegrōtī deam Sūlem adōrāre solēbant. rēx Cogidubnus
cum multīs prīncipibus servīsque prō templō sedēbat. Quīntus
prope sellam rēgis stābat. rēgem prīncipēsque manus mīlitum
custōdiēbat. prō templō erat āra ingēns, quam omnēs aspiciēbant. 5
Memor, togam praetextam gerēns, prope āram stābat.

duo sacerdōtēs, agnam nigram dūcentēs, ad āram prōcessērunt.
postquam rēx signum dedit, ūnus sacerdōs agnam sacrificāvit.
deinde Memor, quī iam tremēbat sūdābatque, alterī sacerdōtī dīxit,
     'iubeō tē ōmina īnspicere. dīc mihi: quid vidēs?'   10
     sacerdōs, postquam iecur agnae īnspexit, anxius,
     'iecur est līvidum', inquit. 'nōnne hoc mortem significat? nōnne
mortem virī clārī significat?'
     Memor, quī perterritus pallēscēbat, sacerdōtī respondit,
     'minimē! dea Sūlis, quae precēs aegrōtōrum audīre solet, nōbīs 15
ōmina optima mīsit.'
     haec verba locūtus, ad Cogidubnum sē vertit et clāmāvit,
     'ōmina sunt optima! ōmina tibi remedium mīrābile significant,
quod dea Sūlis Minerva tibi favet.'
     tum rēgem ac prīncipēs Memor in apodytērium dūxit.   20

manus mīlitum *a band of soldiers*
aspiciēbant: aspicere *look towards*
praetextam: praetextus *with a purple border*
agnam: agna *lamb*
ōmina *omens (signs from the gods)*
iecur *liver*
līvidum: līvidus *lead-coloured*
significat: significāre *mean, indicate*
pallēscēbat: pallēscere *grow pale*
ac *and*

II

deinde omnēs in eam partem thermārum intrāvērunt, ubi balneum
maximum erat. Quīntus, prīncipēs secūtus, circumspectāvit et
attonitus dīxit,
   'hae thermae maiōrēs sunt quam thermae Pompēiānae!'
   servī cum magnā difficultāte Cogidubnum in balneum dēmittere 5
coepērunt. maximus clāmor erat. rēx prīncipibus mandāta dabat.
prīncipēs lībertōs suōs vituperābant, lībertī servōs.
   tandem rēx, ē balneō ēgressus, vestīmenta, quae servī tulerant,
induit. tum omnēs fontī sacrō appropinquāvērunt.
   'ubi est pōculum?' rogāvit Cogidubnus. 'nōbīs decōrum est 10
aquam sacram bibere. aqua est amāra, sed remedium potentis-
simum.'

secūtus *having followed*
difficultāte: difficultās *difficulty*
dēmittere *let down, lower*
amāra: amārus *bitter*

haec verba locūtus, rēx ad fontem sacrum prōcessit. Cephalus, quī anxius tremēbat, prope fontem stābat, pōculum ōrnātissimum tenēns. rēgī pōculum obtulit. rēx pōculum ad labra sustulit. subitō 15 Quīntus, pōculum cōnspicātus, manum rēgis prēnsāvit et clāmāvit,

'nōlī bibere! hoc est pōculum venēnātum. pōculum huius modī in urbe Alexandrīā vīdī.'

'longē errās', respondit rēx. 'nēmō mihi nocēre vult. nēmō umquam mortem mihi parāre temptāvit.' 20

'rēx summae virtūtis es', respondit Quīntus. 'sed, quamquam nūllum perīculum timēs, tūtius est tibi vērum scīre. pōculum īnspicere velim. dā mihi!'

tum pōculum Quīntus īnspicere coepit. Cephalus tamen pōculum ē manibus Quīntī rapere temptābat. maxima pars 25 spectātōrum stābat immōta. sed Dumnorix, prīnceps Rēgnēnsium, saeviēbat tamquam leō furēns. pōculum rapuit et Cephalō obtulit.

'facile est nōbīs vērum cognōscere', clāmāvit. 'iubeō tē pōculum haurīre. num aquam bibere timēs?'

Cephalus pōculum haurīre nōluit, et ad genua rēgis prōcubuit. 30 rēx immōtus stābat. cēterī prīncipēs lībertum frūstrā resistentem prēnsāvērunt. Cephalus, ā prīncipibus coāctus, venēnum hausit. deinde, vehementer tremēns, gemitum ingentem dedit et mortuus prōcubuit.

labra *lips*
prēnsāvit: prēnsāre *take hold of, clutch*
genua *knees*
coāctus: cōgere *force, compel*

epistula Cephalī

postquam Cephalus periit, servus eius rēgī epistulam trādidit, ā
Cephalō ipsō scrīptam:
'rēx Cogidubne, in maximō perīculō es. Memor īnsānit. mortem
tuam cupit. iussit mē rem efficere. invītus Memorī pāruī. fortasse
mihi nōn crēdis. sed tōtam rem tibi nārrāre velim.   5
    ubi tū ad hās thermās advēnistī, remedium quaerēns, Memor mē
ad vīllam suam arcessīvit. vīllam ingressus, Memorem perterritum
invēnī. attonitus eram. numquam Memorem adeō perterritum
vīderam. Memor mihi,
    "Imperātor mortem Cogidubnī cupit", inquit. "iubeō tē hanc 10
rem administrāre. iubeō tē venēnum parāre. tibi necesse est eum
interficere. Cogidubnus enim est homō ingeniī prāvī."
    Memorī respondī,
    "longē errās. Cogidubnus est vir ingeniī optimī. tālem rem facere
nōlō."   15
    Memor īrātus mihi respondit,
    "sceleste! lībertus meus es, et servus meus erās. tē līberāvī et
multam pecūniam dedī. mandāta mea facere dēbēs. cūr mihi
obstās?"
    rēx Cogidubne, diū recūsāvī obstinātus. diū beneficia tua 20
commemorāvī. tandem Memor custōdem arcessīvit, quī mē
verberāvit. ā custōde paene interfectus, Memorī tandem cessī.
    ad casam meam regressus, venēnum invītus parāvī. scrīpsī tamen
hanc epistulam et servō fidēlī trādidī. iussī servum tibi epistulam
trādere. veniam petō, quamquam facinus scelestum parāvī. Memor 25
nocēns est. Memor coēgit mē hanc rem efficere. Memorem, nōn mē,
pūnīre dēbēs.'

īnsānit: īnsānīre *be mad, be insane*
beneficia *acts of kindness, favours*
facinus *crime*
coēgit: cōgere *force, compel*

About the language

1   You have now met the plural of neuter nouns like 'templum' and 'nōmen':

sunt multa **templa** in hāc urbe.
There are many temples in this city.

lībertus **nōmina** prīncipum recitāvit.
The freedman read out the names of the chieftains.

2   Study the nominative and accusative forms of the following neuter nouns:

	singular		*plural*	
	nominative	*accusative*	*nominative*	*accusative*
2nd declension	templum	templum	templa	templa
	aedificium	aedificium	aedificia	aedificia
3rd declension	nōmen	nōmen	nōmina	nōmina
	caput	caput	capita	capita
	mare	mare	maria	maria

3   Further examples:

1   aedificium erat splendidissimum.
2   ubi haec verba audīvit, Memor tacēbat.
3   fēlēs caput hominis rāsit.
4   Cephalus cōnsilium subitō cēpit.
5   haec cubicula sunt sordidissima.
6   servī pōcula ad prīncipēs tulērunt.

When you have read this, answer the questions at the end.

Britannia perdomita

Salvius cum Memore anxius colloquium habet. servus ingressus ad Memorem currit.

servus: domine, rēx Cogidubnus hūc venit. rēx togam praetextam ōrnāmentaque gerit. magnum numerum mīlitum sēcum dūcit.   5

Memor: rēx mīlitēs hūc dūcit? togam praetextam gerit?

Salvius: Cogidubnus, nōs suspicātus, ultiōnem petit. Memor, tibi necesse est mē adiuvāre. nōs enim Rōmānī sumus, Cogidubnus barbarus.

                (intrat Cogidubnus. in manibus epistulam tenet, ā Cephalō 10
                scrīptam.)

Cogidubnus: Memor, tū illās īnsidiās parāvistī. tū iussistī Cephalum venēnum comparāre et mē necāre. sed Cephalus, lībertus tuus, mihi omnia patefēcit.

Memor: Cogidubne, id quod dīcis, absurdum est. mortuus est 15 Cephalus.

perdomita: perdomitus *conquered*
suspicātus *having suspected*
ultiōnem: ultiō *revenge*
patefēcit: patefacere *reveal*
absurdum: absurdus *absurd*

DE BRITANNIS

Cogidubnus: Cephalus homō magnae prūdentiae erat. tibi nōn
crēdidit. invītus tibi pāruit. simulac mandāta ista
dedistī, scrīpsit Cephalus epistulam in quā omnia
patefēcit. servus, ā Cephalō missus, epistulam mihi 20
tulit.
Memor: epistula falsa est, servus mendācissimus.
Cogidubnus: tū, nōn servus, es mendāx. servus enim, multa
tormenta passus, in eādem sententiā mānsit.
Salvius: Cogidubne, cūr mīlitēs hūc dūxistī? 25
Cogidubnus: Memorem ē cūrā thermārum iam dēmōvī.
Memor: quid dīcis? tū mē dēmōvistī? innocēns sum. Salv- . . .
Salvius: rēx Cogidubne, quid fēcistī? tū, quī barbarus es,
haruspicem Rōmānum dēmovēre audēs? nimium
audēs! tū, summōs honōrēs ā nōbīs adeptus, 30
numquam contentus fuistī. nōs diū vexāvistī. nunc
dēnique, cum mīlitibus hūc ingressus, perfidiam
apertē ostendis. Imperātor Domitiānus, arrogantiam
tuam diū passus, ad mē epistulam nūper mīsit. in hāc
epistulā iussit mē rēgnum tuum occupāre. iubeō tē 35
igitur ad aulam statim redīre.
Cogidubnus: ēn iūstitia Rōmāna! ēn fidēs! nūllī perfidiōrēs sunt
quam Rōmānī. stultissimus fuī, quod Rōmānīs adhūc
crēdidī. amīcōs meōs prōdidī; rēgnum meum āmīsī.
ōlim, ā Rōmānīs dēceptus, ōrnāmenta honōrēsque 40
Rōmānōs accēpī. hodiē ista ōrnāmenta, mihi ā
Rōmānīs data, humī iaciō. Salvī, mitte nūntium ad
istum Imperātōrem, 'nōs Cogidubnum tandem
vīcimus. Britannia perdomita est.'
(*senex, haec locūtus, lentē per iānuam exit.*) 45

falsa: falsus *false, untrue*	rēgnum *kingdom*
tormenta *torture*	occupāre *seize, take over*
passus *having suffered*	ēn iūstitia! *so this is justice!*
eādem *the same*	fidēs *loyalty, trustworthiness*
dēmōvī: dēmovēre *dismiss*	perfidiōrēs: perfidus *treacherous, untrustworthy*
perfidiam: perfidia *treachery*	adhūc *up till now*
apertē *openly*	prōdidī: prōdere *betray*
	vīcimus: vincere *conquer*

1 When Memor and Salvius hear of Cogidubnus' arrival, do they think this is an ordinary visit, or a special one? What makes them think so?
2 What reason does Salvius give for saying that Memor ought to support him against Cogidubnus?
3 How has Cogidubnus found out about the poison plot?
4 What action has Cogidubnus taken against Memor? Was this action wise or foolish?
5 Which word in line 29 is used by Salvius to contrast with 'barbarus' in line 28?
6 What orders does Salvius say he has recently received? From whom?
7 Why does Cogidubnus fling his 'ōrnāmenta' to the ground?

Practising the language

1 Study the form and meaning of the following verbs and nouns, and give the meaning of the untranslated words. The verb is given in its infinitive form; sometimes the perfect passive participle has been added in brackets.

arāre	to plough	arātor	ploughman
pingere (pictus)	to paint	pictor	painter
vincere (victus)	to win	victor	
emere (ēmptus)		ēmptor	buyer, purchaser
praecurrere	to run ahead	praecursor	
dūcere (ductus)	to lead	ductor	
legere (lēctus)		lēctor	reader
gubernāre	to steer	gubernātor	
amāre	to love	amātor	
spectāre		spectātor	
favēre		fautor	
		(*written in early Latin as* 'favitor')	

Give the meaning of the following nouns:

dēfēnsor, oppugnātor, vēnditor, saltātor, prōditor

2 Complete each sentence with the right word and then translate.

1 nōs ancillae fessae sumus; semper in vīllā . . . . . .
(labōrāmus, labōrātis, labōrant)

2 'quid faciunt illī servī?' 'saxa ad plaustrum . . . . . .' (ferimus,
fertis, ferunt)

3 fīlius meus vōbīs grātiās agere vult, quod mē . . . . . .
(servāvimus, servāvistis, servāvērunt)

4 quamquam prope āram . . . . ., sacrificium vidēre nōn
poterāmus. (stābāmus, stābātis, stābant)

5 ubi prīncipēs fontī . . . . ., Cephalus prōcessit, pōculum
tenēns. (appropinquābāmus, appropinquābātis, appropinquābant)

6 in maximō perīculō estis, quod fīlium rēgis . . . . . .
(interfēcimus, interfēcistis, interfēcērunt)

7 nōs, quī fontem sacrum numquam . . . . ., ad thermās cum
rēge īre cupiēbāmus. (vīderāmus, vīderātis, vīderant)

8 dominī nostrī sunt benignī; nōbīs semper satis cibī . . . . . .
(praebēmus, praebētis, praebent)

3 Translate the verbs in the left-hand column then, keeping the
person and number unchanged, use the verb in brackets to form
a phrase with the infinitive and translate again. For example:

respondēmus.　(volō)　This becomes:　respondēre volumus.
We reply.　　　　　　　　　　　　　We want to reply.
festīnat.　　　(dēbeō)　This becomes:　festīnāre dēbet.
He hurries.　　　　　　　　　　　　He ought to hurry.

The present tense of 'volō' and 'possum' is set out on page 18 of
the Language Information pamphlet; 'dēbeō' is a second
conjugation verb like 'doceō' (see Language Information
pamphlet, p.14).

1 dormītis.　　(dēbeō)
2 sedēmus.　　(volō)
3 pugnat.　　　(possum)
4 labōrant.　　(dēbeō)
5 revenīmus.　(possum)
6 num nāvigās? (volō)

4 Complete each sentence with the most suitable participle from the list below and then translate.

locūtus, ingressus, missus, excitātus, superātus

1 Cogidubnus, haec verba . . . . ., ab aulā discessit.
2 nūntius, ab amīcīs meīs . . . . ., epistulam mihi trādidit.
3 fūr, vīllam . . . . ., cautē circumspectāvit.
4 Bulbus, ā Modestō . . . . ., sub mēnsā iacēbat.
5 haruspex, ā Cephalō . . . . ., invītus ē lectō surrēxit.

Roman religion

The stories in Stages 22 and 23 have mentioned two ways in which religion played a part in Roman life. In Stage 22, Bulbus sought the help of the gods against his enemy Modestus by means of a defixio; in Stage 23, Memor has been carrying out his duties as a 'haruspex' or soothsayer, by supervising a sacrifice and ordering the examination of the victim's internal organs (entrails). This was one of the ways in which the Romans tried to foretell the future and discover what the gods had in store for them. An invalid hoping for a cure, a general about to fight a battle, and a merchant just before a long business journey, might all consult a haruspex to try to discover their chances of success.

An animal would be sacrificed to the appropriate god or goddess; it was hoped that this would please the god and encourage him to look favourably on the sacrificer. The haruspex and his assistants would make careful observations. They would watch the way in which the victim fell; they would observe the smoke and flames when parts of the victim were placed on the altar fire; and, above all, they would cut the victim open and examine its entrails, especially the liver. They would look for anything unusual about the liver's size or shape, observe its colour and texture and note whether it had spots on its surface. They would then interpret what they saw and announce to the sacrificer whether the signs from the gods were favourable or not.

Bronze liver marked with the different areas to be observed by the haruspex

Such attempts to discover the future were known as divination. Another type of divination was performed by priests known as augurs who based their predictions on observations of the flight of birds. They would note the direction of flight, and observe whether the birds flew together or separately, what kind of birds they were and what noises they made.

Roman religion involved many other beliefs, habits and ceremonies, and it developed over many centuries. The early Romans, in common with many primitive peoples, believed that all things were controlled by spirits which they called 'nūmina'. They had looked at fire and been terrified by its power to burn and destroy, yet excited by its power to cook, warm and provide light. They had seen the regular sequence of day and night and of the seasons of the year but were unable to explain their causes scientifically. Not surprisingly, therefore, they believed that the power of numina was at work, and they soon realised it was important to ensure that the numina used their power for good rather than harm. For this reason the early Romans presented them with offerings of food and wine. At special times of the year, such as seed-time or harvest, an animal would be slaughtered and offered as a sacrifice to the numina. In this way ceremonies and rituals developed at fixed points in the year and gradually communities began to construct calendars to record them.

When the Romans came into contact with the peoples of the Greek world, they began to realise that their own vague and shapeless spirits were imagined by the Greeks as all-powerful gods and goddesses who had not only names and physical shapes but also human characteristics. The Roman corn-spirit, Ceres, became identified with the Greek goddess, Demeter, mother of all life-giving nourishment. The Greeks told stories (myths) about their gods and goddesses which helped to explain more vividly the workings of the world. For example, they said that Demeter's daughter, Persephone, had been carried off by her wicked uncle, Dis, ruler of the Underworld, and was only allowed to return to the earth for six months of the year. In this way a myth was used to explain the rebirth of nature each spring: as Persephone returned each year, Demeter stopped grieving and allowed life back to the countryside.

The Romans were also in contact with the Etruscans, a powerful race who lived in central Italy to the north of Rome. From them they borrowed the practice of divination, described above.

The worship of the gods and goddesses and the practice of divination became central features of the Roman state religion. The rituals and ceremonies were organised by colleges of priests and other religious officials, and the festivals and sacrifices were carried out by them on behalf of the state. The emperor always held the position of 'Pontifex Maximus' or Chief Priest. Great attention was paid to the details of worship. Every word had to be pronounced correctly, otherwise the whole ceremony had to be restarted; a pipe-player was employed to drown noises and cries which were thought to be unlucky for the ritual. Everyone who watched the ceremonies had to stand quite still and silent, like Plancus in the Stage 17 story.

In addition to these public ceremonies, many citizens kept up the practice of private family worship. This included offerings to Vesta, the spirit of the hearth, and to the lares and penates, the spirits of the household and store-cupboard. Such practices were probably more common in the country districts than they were in Rome itself. The head of the household (paterfamiliās) was responsible for performing the rituals and chanting the prayers. Even here everything had to be done correctly and many Roman prayers are worded to make sure that no god or goddess was forgotten or missed out by mistake. It was important to address the god or goddess by the right name, as in this example from a poem by Catullus:

> You are called Juno Lucina
> by women in childbirth,
> you are called nightly Trivia, and Luna
> whose light is not your own.
> . . . may you be hallowed
> by whatever name pleases you . . .

Catullus was, in fact, addressing the goddess Diana, but he used some of her other names to make sure she would attend to his prayer.

The Romans tended to regard prayer as a means of asking for favours from the gods and accompanied their prayers with promises of offerings if the favours were granted. These promises were known as 'vōta'. It would not be an exaggeration to say that many Romans saw religion as a kind of 'business deal' with the gods. A common phrase in prayers was: 'dō ut dēs' – 'I give so that you may give'.

When the Romans arrived in Britain, they found that the Celtic religion was very similar to their own earlier belief in numina. Under Roman influence, the Celts began to identify their spirits with the Roman gods and goddesses, just as the Romans had adopted the Greek gods and goddesses several centuries earlier. The following inscription is a good example of this: 'Peregrinus, son of Secundus, a Treveran, to Mars Loucetius and Nemetona willingly and with good cause fulfilled his vow.' The Roman god Mars and the Celtic god Loucetius are presented here as one god with one name, just as Sulis and Minerva had merged into one goddess at Aquae Sulis. The Romans made no attempt to convert the Celts to a belief in Roman religion. However, they knew that by identifying Roman gods with Celtic ones, they would encourage the British to accept Roman rule more readily.

Another feature of Roman religion which was intended to

Head of the goddess Minerva

encourage acceptance of Roman rule was the worship of the
emperor. In Rome itself, emperor worship was officially
discouraged. However, the peoples of the eastern provinces of the
Roman empire had always regarded their kings and rulers as divine
and were equally ready to pay divine honours to the Roman
emperors. Gradually the Romans introduced this idea in the west as
well. The Britons and other western peoples were encouraged to
worship the 'genius' (protecting spirit) of the emperor, linked with
the goddess Roma. Altars were erected in honour of 'Rome and the
emperor'. When an emperor died it was usual to deify him (make
him a god), and temples were often built to honour the deified
emperor in the provinces. One such temple, that of Claudius in
Colchester, was destroyed by the British before it was even finished,
during the revolt led by Queen Boudica in A.D. 60. The historian

Tacitus tells us why:

'The temple dedicated to the deified Emperor Claudius seemed to the British a symbol of everlasting oppression, and the chosen priests used religion as an excuse for wasting British money.'

Clearly the British found it hard to accept the idea of emperor worship at first.

Words and phrases checklist

administrō, administrāre, administrāvī – look after, manage

cēdō, cēdere, cessī – give in, give way

clārus, clāra, clārum – famous

commemorō, commemorāre, commemorāvī, commemorātus – mention, recall

cōnspicātus, cōnspicāta, cōnspicātum – having caught sight of

cūra, cūrae – care

enim – for

errō, errāre, errāvī – make a mistake

gerō, gerere, gessī, gestus – wear

honor, honōris – honour

iaciō, iacere, iēcī, iactus – throw

immōtus, immōta, immōtum – still, motionless

induō, induere, induī, indūtus – put on

ingenium, ingeniī – character

locūtus, locūta, locūtum – having spoken

mandātum, mandātī – instruction, order

modus, modī – manner, way, kind
    rēs huius modī – a thing of this kind

nimium – too much

numerus, numerī – number

ōrnō, ōrnāre, ōrnāvī, ōrnātus – decorate

pāreō, pārēre, pāruī – obey

potēns, *gen.* potentis – powerful

prāvus, prāva, prāvum – evil

regressus, regressa, regressum – having returned

scio, scīre, scīvī – know

tālis, tāle – such

tamquam – as, like

umquam – ever

venēnum, venēnī – poison

venia, veniae – mercy

fuga

in itinere

Modestus et Strȳthiō, ex oppidō Aquīs Sūlis ēgressī, Dēvam equitābant. in itinere ad flūmen altum vēnērunt, ubi erat pōns sēmirutus. cum ad pontem vēnissent, equus trānsīre nōluit.

'equus trānsīre timet', inquit Modestus. 'Strȳthiō, tū prīmus trānsī!'   5

cum Strȳthiō trānsiisset, equus trānsīre etiam tum nōlēbat. Modestus igitur ex equō dēscendit. cum dēscendisset, equus statim trānsiit.

'eque! redī!' inquit Modestus. 'mē dēseruistī.'

equus tamen in alterā rīpā immōtus stetit. Modestus cautissimē 10 trānsīre coepit. cum ad medium pontem vēnisset, dēcidit pōns, dēcidit Modestus. mediīs ex undīs clāmāvit,

'caudicēs, vōs pontem labefēcistis.'

Dēvam *to Chester*   sēmirutus *rickety*
altum: altus *deep*   labefēcistis: labefacere *weaken*

When you have read this story, answer the questions at the end.

Quīntus cōnsilium capit

cum Cogidubnus trīstis īrātusque ē vīllā Memoris exiisset, Salvius
mīlitēs quīnquāgintā arcessīvit. eōs iussit rēgem prīncipēsque
Rēgnēnsium comprehendere et in carcere retinēre. hī mīlitēs, tōtum
per oppidum missī, mox rēgem cum prīncipibus invēnērunt. eōs
statim comprehendērunt. Dumnorix tamen, ē manibus mīlitum 5
ēlāpsus, per viās oppidī noctū prōcessit et Quīntum quaesīvit.
Quīntō enim crēdēbat.

cubiculum Quīntī ingressus, haec dīxit:

'amīce, tibi crēdere possum. adiuvā mē, adiuvā Cogidubnum.
paucīs Rōmānīs crēdō; plūrimī sunt perfidī. nēmō quidem perfidior 10
est quam iste Salvius quī Cogidubnum interficere nūper temptāvit.
nunc Cogidubnus, ā mīlitibus Salviī comprehēnsus, in carcere iacet.
Salvius crīmen maiestātis in eum īnferre cupit. rēx, in carcere
inclūsus, omnīnō dē vītā suā dēspērat.

'tū tamen es vir summae virtūtis magnaeque prūdentiae. 15
quamquam Salvius potentissimus et īnfestissimus est, nōlī rēgem
dēserere. nōlī eum, ab homine scelestō oppugnātum, relinquere. tū
anteā eum servāvistī. nōnne iterum servāre potes?'

cum Dumnorix haec dīxisset, Quīntus rem sēcum anxius
cōgitābat. auxilium Cogidubnō ferre volēbat, quod eum valdē 20
dīligēbat; sed rēs difficillima erat. subitō cōnsilium cēpit.

'nōlī dēspērāre!' exclāmāvit. 'rēgī auxilium ferre possumus. hanc
rem ad lēgātum Gnaeum Iūlium Agricolam clam referre dēbēmus.
itaque nōbīs festīnandum est ad ultimās partēs Britanniae ubi
Agricola bellum gerit. eī vēra patefacere possumus. Agricola sōlus 25
Salviō obstāre potest, quod summam potestātem in Britanniā
habet. nunc nōbīs hinc effugiendum est.'

Dumnorix, cum haec audīvisset, cōnsilium audāx magnopere
laudāvit. tum Quīntus servum fidissimum arcessīvit, cui mandāta
dedit. servus exiit. mox regressus, cibum sex diērum Quīntō et 30

Dumnorigī trādidit. illī, ē vīllā ēlāpsī, per viās dēsertās cautē prōcessērunt.

vīllam Memoris praetereuntēs, Quīntus et Dumnorix duōs equōs cōnspexērunt, ad pālum dēligātōs. Quīntus, quī fūrtum committere nōlēbat, haesitāvit.   35

Dumnorix rīdēns 'nōlī haesitāre', inquit. 'hī sunt equī Salviī.'

Quīntus et Dumnorix equōs cōnscendērunt et ad ultimās partēs īnsulae abiērunt.

carcere: carcer *prison*
ēlāpsus *having escaped*
quidem *indeed*
crīmen maiestātis *charge of treason*
īnferre *bring against*
inclūsus *shut up, imprisoned*
omnīnō *completely*
sēcum . . . cōgitābat *considered*
   . . . to himself
dīligēbat: dīligere *be fond of*
nōbīs festīnandum est *we must hurry*
ultimās: ultimus *furthest*
bellum gerit: bellum gerere *wage war,*
   campaign

potestātem: potestās *power*
magnopere *greatly*
fīdissimum: fīdus *trustworthy*
diērum: diēs *day*
praetereuntēs: praeterīre *pass by,*
   go past
pālum: pālus *stake, post*
fūrtum *theft, robbery*
committere *commit*
haesitāvit: haesitāre *hesitate*
cōnscendērunt: cōnscendere *mount,*
   climb on

1 How many soldiers does Salvius send for? What does he tell them to do?   *50*

2 Which British chieftain escapes? Whose help does he seek, and why?

3 What further action does Salvius intend to take against Cogidubnus?

4 What events is Dumnorix referring to when he says 'tū anteā eum servāvistī' (lines 17–18)?

5 What does Quintus suggest? Why does he think Agricola can stop Salvius?

6 How many days' food do Quintus and Dumnorix take with them? How do they obtain horses?

7 Why does Quintus support a British king and a British chieftain, instead of supporting his fellow-Roman Salvius?

About the language

1   Study the following sentences:

cum Modestus ad pontem **advēnisset**, equus cōnstitit.
When Modestus had arrived at the bridge, the horse stopped.

cum coquus omnia **parāvisset**, mercātor amīcōs in triclīnium
dūxit.
When the cook had got everything ready, the merchant led his
friends into the dining-room.

The form of the verb in heavy print is known as the *subjunctive*.

2   The subjunctive is often used with the word 'cum' meaning
'when', as in the examples above.

3   Further examples:

1   cum rēx exiisset, Salvius mīlitēs ad sē vocāvit.
2   cum gladiātōrēs leōnem interfēcissent, spectātōrēs
    plausērunt.
3   cum dominus haec mandāta dedisset, fabrī ad aulam
    rediērunt.
4   fūrēs, cum cubiculum intrāvissent, tacitī circumspectāv-
    ērunt.

4   The examples of the subjunctive in paragraphs 1 and 3 are all in
the same tense: the *pluperfect subjunctive*. Compare the pluperfect
subjunctive with the ordinary form of the pluperfect:

pluperfect	*pluperfect subjunctive*	
3rd person singular	*3rd person singular*	*3rd person plural*
trāxerat	trāxisset	trāxissent
ambulāverat	ambulāvisset	ambulāvissent
dormīverat	dormīvisset	dormīvissent
voluerat	voluisset	voluissent
fuerat	fuisset	fuissent

Salvius cōnsilium cognōscit

postrīdiē mīlitēs Dumnorigem per oppidum quaerēbant. cum eum
nusquam invenīre potuissent, rem dēnique Salviō nūntiāvērunt.
ille, cum dē fugā Dumnorigis cognōvisset, vehementer saeviēbat;
omnēs mīlitēs, quī Dumnorigem custōdīverant, poenās dare iussit.
Quīntum quoque quaesīvit; invenīre tamen nōn poterat. tum 5
Belimicum, prīncipem Canticōrum, arcessīvit.

'Belimice', inquit, 'iste Dumnorix ē manibus meīs effūgit; abest
quoque Quīntus Caecilius. neque Dumnorigī neque Quīntō crēdō.
Quīntus enim saepe Dumnorigī favēbat, saepe cum eō colloquium
habēbat. ī nunc; dūc mīlitēs tēcum; illōs quaere in omnibus partibus 10

nusquam *nowhere* fugā: fuga *escape* ī: īre *go*

oppidī. quaere servōs quoque eōrum. facile est nōbīs servōs torquēre et vērum ita cognōscere.'

Belimicus, multīs cum mīlitibus ēgressus, per oppidum dīligenter quaerēbat. intereā Salvius anxius reditum eius exspectābat. cum Salvius rem sēcum cōgitāret, Belimicus subitō rediit exsultāns. servum Quīntī in medium ātrium trāxit.

'fūgērunt illī scelestī', clāmāvit, 'sed hic servus, captus et interrogātus, vērum patefēcit.'

Salvius ad servum trementem conversus,

'ubi est Quīntus Caecilius?' inquit. 'quō fūgit Dumnorix?'

'nescio', inquit servus quī, multa tormenta passus, iam vix quicquam dīcere poterat. 'nihil scio', iterum inquit.

Belimicus, cum haec audīvisset, gladium dēstrictum ad iugulum servī tenuit.

'melius est tibi', inquit, 'vērum Salviō dīcere.'

servus quī iam dē vītā suā dēspērābat,

'cibum sex diērum tantum parāvī', inquit susurrāns. 'nihil aliud fēcī. dominus meus cum Dumnorige in ultimās partēs Britanniae discessit.'

Salvius 'hercle!' inquit. 'ad Agricolam iērunt. Quīntus, ā Dumnorige incitātus, mihi obstāre temptat; homō tamen magnae stultitiae est; mihi resistere nōn potest, quod ego maiōrem auctōritātem habeō quam ille.'

Salvius, cum haec dīxisset, Belimicō mandāta dedit. eum iussit cum ducentīs equitibus exīre et fugitīvōs comprehendere. servum carnificibus trādidit. deinde scrībam arcessīvit cui epistulam dictāvit. ūnum ē servīs suīs iussit hanc epistulam quam celerrimē ad Agricolam ferre.

intereā Belimicus, Quīntum et Dumnorigem per multōs diēs secūtus, eōs tandem invēnit. equitēs statim impetum in eōs fēcērunt. amīcī, ab equitibus circumventī, fortiter resistēbant. dēnique Dumnorix humī cecidit mortuus; Quīntus vulnerātus magnā cum difficultāte effūgit.

torquēre *torture*	quicquam *anything*
reditum: reditus *return*	dēstrictum: dēstringere *draw*
exsultāns: exsultāre *exult, be triumphant*	iugulum *throat*
conversus *having turned*	fugitīvōs: fugitīvus *fugitive*
	scrībam: scrība *secretary*

About the language

1   At the beginning of this Stage, you met sentences with 'cum' and the *pluperfect subjunctive*:

senex, cum pecūniam **invēnisset**, ad vīllam laetus rediit.
When the old man had found the money, he returned happily to the villa.

cum rem **cōnfēcissent**, abiērunt.
When they had finished the job, they went away.

2   Now study the following examples:

cum custōdēs **dormīrent**, captīvī ē carcere effūgērunt.
When the guards were sleeping, the prisoners escaped from the prison.

Modestus, cum in Britanniā **mīlitāret**, multās puellās amābat.
When Modestus was serving in the army in Britain, he loved many girls.

In these sentences, 'cum' is being used with a different tense of the subjunctive: the *imperfect subjunctive*.

3   Further examples:

1 cum hospitēs cēnam cōnsūmerent, fūr cubiculum intrāvit.
2 cum prīnceps rem cōgitāret, nūntiī subitō revēnērunt.
3 iuvenēs, cum bēstiās agitārent, mīlitem vulnerātum cōnspexērunt.
4 puella, cum epistulam scrīberet, sonitum mīrābilem audīvit.

4   Compare the imperfect subjunctive with the infinitive:

infinitive	*imperfect subjunctive*	
	3rd person singular	*3rd person plural*
trahere	traheret	traherent
ambulāre	ambulāret	ambulārent
dormīre	dormīret	dormīrent
velle	vellet	vellent
esse	esset	essent

67

Practising the language

1 Study the form and meaning of the following, and give the meaning of the untranslated words:

volō	I want	nōlō	I do not want
scīre	to know	nescīre	not to know
umquam	ever	numquam	
usquam	anywhere	nusquam	
fās	right, lawful	nefās	

patiēns		impatiēns	impatient
mortālis		immortālis	
sānus	of sound mind	īnsānus	
memor	remembering	immemor	
fēlīx		īnfēlīx	unlucky
amīcus	friend	inimīcus	
ūtilis		inūtilis	useless
pavidus		impavidus	fearless
nōtus	known, well-known	ignōtus	
aequus	fair, equal	inīquus	

cōnsentīre	to agree	dissentīre	
facilis		difficilis	difficult
similis		dissimilis	unlike

Notice again the meanings of three pairs of words which you have already met:

ōtium	leisure	neg-ōtium	non-leisure, i.e. business
legere	to read, to attend to	neg-legere	not to attend to, i.e. to neglect
homō	man	nēmō	no man, i.e. nobody

Give the meaning of the following words:

immōtus, incertus, incrēdibilis, indignus, ingrātus, nocēns

2 With the help of paragraph 5 on page 11 of the Language
Information pamphlet, replace the words in heavy print with
the correct form of the pronoun 'is' and then translate. For
example:

Rūfilla in hortō ambulābat. Quīntus **Rūfillam** salūtāvit.
This becomes:
Rūfilla in hortō ambulābat. Quīntus eam salūtāvit.
Rufilla was walking in the garden. Quintus greeted her.

In sentences 7 and 8, you may need to look up the gender of a
noun in the 'Words and phrases' section of the Language
Information pamphlet.

1 Quīntus mox ad aulam advēnit. ancilla **Quīntum** in ātrium
   dūxit.
2 Salvius in lectō recumbēbat. puer **Salviō** plūs cibī obtulit.
3 Rūfilla laetissima erat; marītus **Rūfillae** tamen nōn erat
   contentus.
4 Britannī ferōciter pugnāvērunt, sed legiōnēs nostrae tandem
   Britannōs vīcērunt.
5 barbarī impetum in nōs fēcērunt. **barbarīs** autem restitimus.
6 multae fēminae prō templō conveniēbant. līberī **fēminārum**
   quoque aderant.
7 in illō oppidō est fōns sacer; **fontem** saepe vīsitāvī.
8 in Britanniā sunt trēs legiōnēs; imperātor **legiōnēs** iussit
   barbarōs vincere.

3 Complete each sentence with the right word and then translate.

1 subitō ancilla . . . . . in ātrium irrūpit. (perterrita, perterritae)
2 rēx, postquam hoc audīvit, fabrōs . . . . . dīmīsit. (fessum,
   fessōs)
3 centuriō quī adstābat custōdēs . . . . . laudāvit. (callidum,
   callidōs)
4 omnēs cīvēs nāvem . . . . . spectābant. (sacram, sacrās)
5 ubi in magnō perīculō eram, amīcus . . . . . mē servāvit.
   (fidēlis, fidēlēs)
6 'in illā īnsulā', inquit senex, 'habitant multī virī . . . . . .'
   (ferōx, ferōcēs)

4 Make up six Latin sentences using some of the words listed below. Write out each sentence and then translate it. Include *two* sentences which do not contain nominatives.

nominatives	accusatives	datives	verbs
senātor	flōrēs	fīliae	emō
centuriōnēs	dōna	uxōrī	emit
prīnceps	gladiōs	mīlitibus	emunt
nūntius	fēlem	agricolae	ostendō
amīcī	plaustra	dominō	ostendit
marītus	vīnum	hospitibus	ostendunt
puella	cibum	fēminīs	dat
iuvenēs	epistulās	imperātōrī	damus
virī	fūrem	carnificibus	dant
ancillae	cēram	servīs	trādit
			trāditis
			trādunt

Travel and communication

Judged by modern Western standards, travelling in the Roman world was neither easy nor comfortable; nevertheless, people travelled extensively and there was much movement of goods throughout the provinces of the empire. This was made possible by a remarkable network of straight, well-surfaced roads which connected all major towns by the shortest possible routes. Travellers went on horseback, or used carts or other wheeled vehicles, or they walked. Such journeys were limited by the freshness of horse or traveller. They could cover 60–70 km (40–50 miles) in a day by carriage, perhaps 35 km (25 miles) on foot.

The line of a Roman road was first laid out by surveyors. By taking sightings from high points using smoke from fires, it was possible to ensure that each section of road took the shortest practicable distance between the points. River valleys and impassable mountains forced the roads to make diversions, but once past the obstructions, the roads usually continued along their original line. After the line had been chosen, an embankment of

Aerial photograph of a Roman road, showing a diversion round a steep-sided valley

Cross-section showing structure of a Roman road

earth, called an 'agger', was raised to act as a firm foundation. An agger could be as high as 1.2–1.5 metres (4–5 feet). In this was embedded a footing of large stones. This was covered with a layer of smaller stones, rubble and hardcore, and the surface was faced with local materials: large flat stones, small flints or slag from iron mines. This final surface is known as metalling and was curved or 'cambered' to provide effective drainage. On either side of the agger, ditches were dug for the same purpose. Roman road-building was generally carried out with great skill and thoroughness, and the remains of a number of roads still exist today. Many modern roads still follow the Roman alignments and these can be seen very clearly on Ordnance Survey maps.

The roads' original purpose was to allow rapid movement of Roman troops and so ensure military control of the provinces. Other travellers included Roman government officials, who made use of a system known as the Imperial Post (cursus pūblicus). A traveller with a government warrant (diplōma) who was making a journey on official business was supplied with fresh horses at posting stations which were sited at frequent intervals along all main roads; every effort was made to speed such a traveller on his way. In particular, the cursus publicus was used for carrying government correspondence. It has been estimated that by means of the cursus publicus an official message could travel from Britain to Rome (a distance of some 1800 kilometres, 1100 miles) in about seven days. Private letters carried by a person's own slave took much longer.

Travellers would break long journeys with overnight stays at roadside inns. These were, for the most part, small, dirty and uncomfortable, and were frequented by thieves, prostitutes and drunks. The innkeepers, too, were often dishonest. The poet Horace, describing his stay at one inn, comments tersely: 'perfidus hic caupō'. Well-to-do travellers would try to avoid using these inns by arranging to stay with friends or acquaintances, where possible.

Relief showing a Roman light-weight carriage approaching a mile stone

Travelling by sea was generally more popular, although it was restricted to the sailing season (March to November) and was fraught with danger from pirates, storms and shipwrecks. Most sea journeys were undertaken on merchant ships; passenger shipping as we know it did not exist, except for the occasional ferry. A traveller could either hire a boat or wait until a merchant ship was about to put to sea and bargain with the captain for an acceptable fare.

Words and phrases checklist

adstō, adstāre, adstitī – stand by
auctōritās, auctōritātis – authority
audāx, *gen.* audācis – bold, daring
carcer, carceris – prison
colloquium, colloquiī – talk, chat
comprehendō, comprehendere, comprehendī, comprehēnsus –
  arrest
cōnscendō, cōnscendere, cōnscendī – climb on, mount
cum – when
dēscendō, dēscendere, dēscendī – go down, come down
dēserō, dēserere, dēseruī, dēsertus – desert
ēgressus, ēgressa, ēgressum – having gone out
eques, equitis – horseman
flūmen, flūminis – river
humī – on the ground
īnfestus, īnfesta, īnfestum – hostile
intereā – meanwhile
magnopere – greatly
  maximē – very greatly, most of all
neque . . . neque – neither . . . nor
nusquam – nowhere
oppugnō, oppugnāre, oppugnāvī, oppugnātus – attack
passus, passa, passum – having suffered
patefaciō, patefacere, patefēcī, patefactus – reveal
perfidus, perfida, perfidum – treacherous, untrustworthy
pōns, pontis – bridge
rīpa, rīpae – river bank
tantum – only
trānseō, trānsīre, trānsiī – cross
trīstis, trīste – sad
vērum, vērī – the truth

mīlitēs

mīles legiōnis secundae per castra ambulābat. subitō iuvenem
ignōtum prope horreum latentem cōnspexit.
'heus tū', clāmāvit mīles, 'quis es?' iuvenis nihil respondit.
mīles iuvenem iterum rogāvit quis esset. iuvenis fūgit.

mīles iuvenem petīvit et facile superāvit. 'furcifer!' exclāmāvit.
'quid prope horreum facis?'
iuvenis dīcere nōlēbat quid prope horreum faceret. mīles eum ad
centuriōnem dūxit.

centuriō, iuvenem cōnspicātus, 'hunc agnōscō!' inquit. 'explōrātor
Britannicus est, quem saepe prope castra cōnspexī. quō modō eum
cēpistī?'
tum mīles explicāvit quō modō iuvenem cēpisset.

centuriō, ad iuvenem conversus, 'cūr in castra vēnistī?' rogāvit.
iuvenis tamen tacēbat.
centuriō, ubi cognōscere nōn poterat cūr iuvenis in castra vēnisset,
mīlitem iussit eum ad carcerem dūcere.

iuvenis, postquam verba centuriōnis audīvit, 'ego sum Vercobrix',
inquit, 'fīlius prīncipis Deceanglōrum. vōbīs nōn decōrum est mē in
carcere tenēre.' 'fīlius prīncipis Deceanglōrum?' exclāmāvit
centuriō. 'libentissimē tē videō. nōs tē diū quaerimus, cellamque
optimam tibi in carcere parāvimus.'

Strȳthiō

optiō per castra ambulat. Strȳthiōnem, iam ad castra regressum, cōnspicit.

optiō: heus Strȳthiō! hūc venī! tibi aliquid dīcere volō.

Strȳthiō: nōlī mē vexāre! occupātus sum. Modestum quaerō, quod puella eum exspectat. hercle! puellam pulchriōrem numquam vīdī. vōx eius est suāvissima; oculī eius . . .   5

optiō: mī Strȳthiō, quamquam occupātissimus es, dēbēs maximā cum dīligentiā mē audīre. ā centuriōne nostrō missus sum. centuriō tē iubet ad carcerem statim festīnāre.

Strȳthiō: īnsānit centuriō! innocēns sum.   10

optiō: tacē! centuriō Modestum quoque iussit ad carcerem festīnāre.

Strȳthiō: deōs testēs faciō. innocentēs sumus. nūllum facinus commīsimus.

optiō: caudex! tacē! difficile est rem tibi explicāre! Valerius, 1 centuriō noster, vōs ambōs carcerem custōdīre iussit.

Strȳthiō: nōlī mē vituperāre! rem nunc intellegō! Valerius nōs vult custōdēs carceris esse. decōrum est Valeriō nōs ēligere, quod fortissimī sumus. ego et Modestus, cum in Āfricā mīlitārēmus, sōlī tōtam prōvinciam custōdiēbāmus.   2

optiō: quamquam fortissimī estis, dīligentiam quoque maximam praestāre dēbētis. nam inter captīvōs est Vercobrix, iuvenis magnae dignitātis, cuius pater est prīnceps Deceanglōrum. necesse est vōbīs Vercobrigem dīligentissimē custōdīre.

optiō *optio (military officer, ranking below centurion)*
castra *camp*
ambōs: ambō *both*
prōvinciam: prōvincia *province*
praestāre *show, display*
captīvōs: captīvus *prisoner, captive*
cuius *whose (genitive of* quī*)*

Strȳthiō: nōlī anxius esse, mī optiō. nōbīs nihil difficile est, quod
fortissimī sumus, ut anteā dīxī. tū redī ad Valerium. dīc
Valeriō haec omnia verba. nōlī quicquam omittere!
'Strȳthiō, mīles legiōnis secundae, Valeriō, centuriōnī
legiōnis secundae, salūtem plūrimam dīcit. optiō, ā tē 30
missus, mandāta tua nōbīs tulit. nōs mandātīs tuīs
pārentēs, ad statiōnem prōcēdimus.'

exeunt. optiō centuriōnem quaerit, Strȳthiō amīcum.

omittere *leave out, omit*
salūtem plūrimam dīcit *sends his best wishes*
pārentēs: pārēre *obey*
statiōnem: statiō *post*

Modestus custōs

Modestus et Strȳthiō, carcerem ingressī, cellās in quibus captīvī erant īnspiciēbant. habēbat Strȳthiō libellum in quō nōmina captīvōrum scrīpta erant. Modestus eum rogāvit in quā cellā Vercobrix inclūsus esset. Strȳthiō, libellum īnspiciēns, cognōvit ubi Vercobrix iacēret, et Modestum ad cellam dūxit. Modestus, cum ad 5 portam cellae advēnisset, haesitāns cōnstitit.

Strȳthiō 'num cellam intrāre timēs?' inquit. 'vīnctus est fīlius prīncipis Deceanglōrum. tē laedere nōn potest.'

cum Strȳthiō haec dīxisset, Modestus īrātus exclāmāvit,

'caudex, prīncipis fīlium nōn timeō! cōnstitī quod tē 10 exspectābam. volō tē mihi portam aperīre!'

cum portam Strȳthiō aperuisset, Modestus rūrsus haesitāvit.

'obscūra est cella', inquit Modestus anxius. 'fer mihi lucernam.'

Strȳthiō, vir summae patientiae, lucernam tulit amīcōque trādidit. ille, cellam ingressus, ē cōnspectū discessit.   15

Medieval Dildo! —Belonging to Quintus' Mum.

in angulō cellae iacēbat Vercobrix. Modestus, cum eum vīdisset, gladium dēstrīnxit. tum, ad mediam cellam prōgressus, Vercobrigem vituperāre coepit. Vercobrix tamen contumēliās Modestī audīre nōn poterat, quod graviter dormiēbat. Modestus Vercobrigī dormientī exsultāns appropinquāvit, et gladium ante ōs 20 eius vibrābat. iterum magnā cum vōce eum vituperābat. Strȳthiō, quī extrā cellam stābat, attonitus erat. nesciēbat enim cūr Modestus clāmāret. dormiēbat tamen Vercobrix, ignārus clāmōrum Modestī.

subitō arānea, ē tēctō cellae lāpsa, in nāsum Modestī incidit et trāns ōs cucurrit. Modestus, ab arāneā territus, ē cellā fūgit.   25

'Strȳthiō! Strȳthiō!' clāmāvit. 'claude portam cellae. nōbīs

necesse est summā cum dīligentiā Vercobrigem custōdīre. etiam
arāneae eum adiuvant!'

Strȳthiō cum portam clausisset, Modestum territum rogāvit quid
accidisset. 30

'Modeste', inquit, 'quam pallidus es! num captīvum timēs?'

'minimē! pallidus sum, quod nōn cēnāvī', respondit.

'vīsne mē ad culīnam īre et tibi cēnam ferre?' rogāvit Strȳthiō.

'optimum cōnsilium est!' inquit alter. 'tū tamen hīc manē. melius
est mihi ipsī ad culīnam īre, quod coquus decem dēnāriōs mihi 35
dēbet.'

haec locūtus, ad culīnam statim cucurrit.

cōnstitit: cōnsistere *halt, stop*
vīnctus: vincīre *bind, tie up*
lucernam: lucerna *lamp*
patientiae: patientia *patience*
cōnspectū: cōnspectus *sight*
angulō: angulus *corner*
prōgressus *having advanced*
contumēliās: contumēlia *insult, abuse*
ante ōs eius *in front of his face*
ignārus *not knowing, unaware*
arānea *spider*
tēctō: tēctum *ceiling, roof*
lāpsa: lāpsus *having fallen*
trāns *across*
pallidus *pale*
hīc *here*

About the language

1   In Unit I, you met sentences like this:

'quis clāmōrem audīvit?'   'ubi est captīvus?'
'Who heard the shout?'   'Where is the prisoner?'

In each example, a question is being *asked*. These examples are known as *direct* questions.

2   In Stage 25, you have met sentences like this:

centuriō nesciēbat quis clāmōrem audīvisset.
The centurion did not know who had heard the shout.

equitēs cognōvērunt ubi captīvus esset.
The horsemen found out where the prisoner was.

In each of these examples, the question is not being asked, but is being *reported* or *mentioned*. These examples are known as *indirect* questions. The verb in an indirect question in Latin is normally subjunctive.

3   Compare the following examples:

direct questions	*indirect questions*
'quid Vercobrix fēcit?'	mīlitēs intellēxērunt quid Vercobrix fēcisset.
'What has Vercobrix done?'	The soldiers understood what Vercobrix had done.
'cūr Britannī fūgērunt?'	optiō rogāvit cūr Britannī fūgissent.
'Why did the Britons run away?'	The optio asked why the Britons had run away.
'quis appropinquat?'	custōs nesciēbat quis appropinquāret.
'Who is approaching?'	The guard did not know who was approaching.

4 Further examples of direct and indirect questions:

1 'quis puerum interfēcit?'
2 nēmō sciēbat quis puerum interfēcisset.
3 Salvius tandem intellēxit quō Quīntus et Dumnorix fūgissent.
4 nūntius scīre voluit ubi rēx habitāret.
5 'quō modō pecūniam invēnistī?'
6 iūdex mē rogāvit quō modō pecūniam invēnissem.
7 Salvius nesciēbat cūr Quīntus rēgem adiūvisset.
8 Salvius nesciēbat cūr Quīntus rēgem adiuvāret.

Modestus perfuga

I

Modestus, ēgressus ē culīnā ubi cēnam optimam cōnsūmpserat, ad carcerem redībat. cum ambulāret, sīc cōgitābat,
'numquam cēnam meliōrem gustāvī; numquam vīnum suāvius bibī. sollicitus tamen sum. nam coquus illam cēnam et mihi et Strȳthiōnī parāvit, sed ego sōlus cōnsūmpsī. nunc mihi necesse est 5
hanc rem Strȳthiōnī explicāre. fortūna tamen mihi favet, quod Strȳthiō est vir magnae patientiae, minimīque cibī.'

perfuga *deserter*
et . . . et *both . . . and*

ubi carcerī appropinquāvit, portam apertam vīdit.

'dī immortālēs!' clāmāvit permōtus. 'Strȳthiō, num portam carceris apertam relīquistī? nēminem neglegentiōrem quam tē nōvī.' 10

carcerem ingressus, portās omnium cellārum apertās invēnit. cum hoc vīdisset, exclāmāvit,

'ēheu! omnēs portae apertae sunt! captīvī, ē cellīs ēlāpsī, omnēs fūgērunt!'

Modestus rem anxius cōgitāvit. nesciēbat enim quō captīvī 15 fūgissent; intellegere nōn poterat cūr Strȳthiō abesset.

'quid facere dēbeō? perīculōsum est hīc manēre ubi mē centuriō invenīre potest. ūna est spēs salūtis. mihi fugiendum est. ō Strȳthiō, Strȳthiō! coēgistī mē statiōnem dēserere. mē perfugam fēcistī. sed deōs testēs faciō. invītus statiōnem dēserō, invītus centuriōnis īram 20 fugiō.'

permōtus *alarmed, disturbed*   spēs *hope*   īram: īra *anger*

II

Modestus, haec locūtus, subitō sonitum audīvit. aliquis portam cellae Vercobrigis aperīre et exīre temptābat!

'mihi ē carcere fugiendum est', aliquis ē cellā clāmāvit.

Modestus, cum haec audīvisset, ad portam cellae cucurrit et clausit. 5

'Vercobrix, tibi in cellā manendum est!' clāmāvit Modestus. 'euge! nōn effūgit Vercobrix! eum captīvum habeō! euge! nunc mihi centuriō nocēre nōn potest, quod captīvum summae dignitātis in carcere retinuī.'

Modestus autem anxius manēbat; nesciēbat enim quid Strȳthiōnī 10 accidisset. subitō pugiōnem humī relictum cōnspexit.

'heus, quid est? hunc pugiōnem agnōscō! est pugiō Strȳthiōnis! Strȳthiōnī dedī, ubi diem nātālem celebrābat. ēheu! cruentus est pugiō. ō mī Strȳthiō! nunc rem intellegō. mortuus es! captīvī, ē cellīs ēlāpsī, tē necāvērunt. ēheu! cum ego tuam cēnam in culīnā 15 cōnsūmerem, illī tē oppugnābant! ō Strȳthiō! nēmō īnfēlīcior est quam ego. nam tē amābam sīcut pater fīlium. tū tamen nōn inultus periistī. Vercobrix, quī in hāc cellā etiam nunc manet, poenās dare dēbet. heus! Vercobrix, mē audī! tibi moriendum est, quod Strȳthiō meus mortuus est.' 20

haec locūtus, in cellam furēns irrūpit. captīvum, quī intus latēbat, verberāre coepit.

captīvus: Modeste! mī Modeste! dēsine mē verberāre! nōnne mē agnōscis? Strȳthiō sum, quem tū amās sīcut pater fīlium. 25

Modestus: Strȳthiō? Strȳthiō! num vīvus es? cūr vīvus es? sceleste! furcifer! ubi sunt captīvī quōs custōdiēbās?

Strȳthiō: fūgērunt, Modeste. mē dēcēpērunt. coēgērunt mē portās omnium cellārum aperīre.

Modestus: ēheu! quid facere dēbēmus? 30

Strȳthiō: nōbīs statim ē carcere fugiendum est; centuriōnem appropinquantem audiō.

Modestus: ō Strȳthiō! ō, quam īnfēlīx sum!

Strȳthiō: nōlī dēspērāre. cōnsilium habeō. tibi necesse est mihi cōnfīdere. 35

amīcī ē carcere quam celerrimē fūgērunt.

---

aliquis *someone*	inultus *unavenged*
relictum: relinquere *leave*	tibi moriendum est *you must die*
cruentus *covered in blood*	vīvus *alive, living*

About the language

1 The examples of the imperfect and pluperfect subjunctive that you have met so far have nearly all ended in '-t' or '-nt', meaning 'he . . .' or 'they . . .':

> nēmō sciēbat ubi Britannī **latērent**.
> Nobody knew where the Britons were lying hidden.

> centuriō, cum hoc **audīvisset**, saeviēbat.
> When the centurion had heard this, he was furious.

2 The imperfect and pluperfect subjunctive can also end in '-m', '-mus', '-s' or '-tis', meaning 'I . . .', 'we . . .' or 'you . . .':

> custōdēs nōs rogāvērunt cūr **clāmārēmus**.
> The guards asked us why we were shouting.

> cum patrem **excitāvissem**, ad cubiculum rediī.
> When I had awakened my father, I returned to my bedroom.

3 Further examples:

 1 nesciēbam quō fūgissēs.
 2 cum in Britanniā mīlitārem, oppidum Aquās Sūlis saepe vīsitāvī.
 3 cum cēnam tuam cōnsūmerēs, centuriō tē quaerēbat.
 4 cum nōmina recitāvissem, hospitēs ad rēgem dūxī.
 5 amīcus meus cognōscere voluit ubi habitārētis.
 6 puella nōs rogāvit cūr rem tam difficilem suscēpissēmus.

4 The imperfect and pluperfect tenses of the subjunctive are set out in full on page 16 of the Language Information pamphlet.

Practising the language

1   Study the form and meaning of the following nouns and give the
    meaning of the untranslated ones:

deus	god	dea	goddess
fīlius	son	fīlia	
ursus		ursa	she-bear
lupus		lupa	
leō		leaena	
captīvus	prisoner (male)	captīva	
avus	grandfather	avia	
saltātor	dancer	saltātrīx	dancing-girl
vēnātor	hunter	vēnātrīx	
victor		victrīx	winner (female)

Give the meaning of the following nouns:

rēgīna, domina, equa, nūntia

2   Complete the sentences of this story with the most suitable word
    from the list below, and then translate.

clāmāvit, cucurrit, invēnit, coxit, bibit, cōnsūmpsit, exiit

Modestus ad culīnam īrātus . . . . . . culīnam ingressus,
coquum occupātum . . . . . . coquus cibum parābat.
    'ubi sunt dēnāriī quōs mihi dēbēs?' . . . . . Modestus.
    coquus, ubi Modestum īrātum vīdit, eī pōculum vīnī obtulit.
Modestus libenter vīnum . . . . . . deinde coquus cēnam
. . . . .et Modestō obtulit. Modestus, simulac cēnam gustāvit,
avidus . . . . . .
    postrēmō Modestus, optimē cēnātus, ē culīnā ēbrius . . . . .,
immemor pecūniae. coquus in culīnā stābat cachinnāns.

3 Translate the following sentences and then, with the help of the tables on pages 4–6 of the Language Information pamphlet, change their meaning by turning each nominative into a dative and each dative into a nominative, then translate again.

For example: imperātor rēgibus dōna dedit.
            The emperor gave gifts to the kings.
This becomes: rēgēs imperātōrī dōna dedērunt.
            The kings gave gifts to the emperor.

Notice that in some sentences, as in the example above, you will have to change the verb from singular to plural, or plural to singular.

1 puella puerō gemmam ostendit.
2 mercātor amīcō dōnum ēmit.
3 servus puellīs respondit.
4 rēx cīvibus haec verba dīxit.
5 puerī cīvī nōn crēdidērunt.
6 mīlitēs fēminīs auxilium dedērunt.
7 custōdēs centuriōnī pecūniam trādidērunt.
8 ego tibi nōn fāvī.

4 This exercise is based on the story 'Modestus custōs' on page 80. Read the story again. Complete each of the sentences below with one of the following groups of words and then translate. Use each group of words once only.

cum Modestus ad culīnam abiisset
cum carcerem intrāvissent
cum arānea dē tēctō dēcidisset
cum lucernam tulisset
cum Modestus gladium vibrāret

1 Modestus et Strȳthiō, ..., cellās captīvōrum īnspiciēbant
2 Strȳthiō, ..., Modestō trādidit.
3 . . . . ., Vercobrix graviter dormiēbat.
4 . . . . ., Modestus fūgit perterritus.
5 . . . . ., Strȳthiō in carcere mānsit.

5 Complete each sentence with the right word and then translate.

1 medicus puellae . . . . . pōculum dedit. (aegram, aegrae)
2 hospitēs coquum . . . . . laudāvērunt. (callidum, callidō)
3 faber mercātōrī . . . . . dēnāriōs reddidit. (īrātum, īrātō)
4 ancillae dominō . . . . . pārēre nōlēbant. (crūdēlem, crūdēlī)
5 centuriō mīlitēs . . . . . castīgābat. (ignāvōs, ignāvīs)
6 puer stultus nautīs . . . . . crēdidit. (mendācēs, mendācibus)
7 stolās . . . . . emēbat fēmina. (novās, novīs)
8 . . . . . amīcīs pecūniam obtulī. (omnēs, omnibus)

The legionary soldier

The crack troops of the Roman army were the soldiers who served in the legions. They were all Roman citizens and full-time professionals who had signed on for twenty-five years. They were highly trained in the skills of infantry warfare and were often specialists in other things as well. In fact a Roman legion, consisting normally of about 5,000 foot soldiers, was a miniature army in itself, capable of constructing forts and camps, manufacturing its weapons and equipment and building roads. On its staff were engineers, architects, carpenters, smiths, doctors, medical orderlies, clerks and accountants.

Recruitment

When he joined the army a new recruit would first be interviewed to ensure that he had the proper legal status, i.e. that he was a Roman citizen; he was also given a medical examination. The army was inclined to favour recruits who came from certain trades, preferring 'blacksmiths, wagon-makers, butchers and huntsmen' and disapproving of 'confectioners, weavers and those who have been employed in occupations appropriate to the women's quarters'.

A legion

First Cohort
5 centuries=*c.* 800 men

Second to Tenth Cohorts
6 centuries each=*c.* 4320 men

O
Ct
about 160 men

O
Ct
about 160 men

O
Ct
about 160 men

O
Ct
about 160 men

O
about 160 men

T S C

PP

PC

aquilifer

legatus

tribuni

O
Ct
about 80 men

O
Ct
about 80 men

O
Ct
about 80 men

O
Ct
about 80 men

O
Ct
about 80 men

O
Ct
about 80 men

T S C

about 120 horsemen

T=tesserarius; S=signifer; C=cornicen (trumpeter); Ct=centurio; O=optio;
PP=primus pilus; PC=praefectus castrorum

Training

After being accepted and sworn in, the new recruit was sent to his unit to begin training. This was thorough, systematic and physically hard. First the young soldier had to learn to march at the regulation pace for distances of up to 24 Roman miles (about 22 statute miles or 35 kilometres). Physical fitness was further developed by running, jumping, swimming and carrying heavy packs. Next came weapon training, starting with a wooden practice-sword and wicker shield. The soldier learned to handle the shield correctly and to attack a dummy target with the point of his sword. When he had mastered the basic skills with dummy weapons he went on to the real thing and finally practised individual combat in pairs, probably with a leather button on the point of his sword.

The second phase of weapon training was to learn to throw the javelin (pīlum). This had a wooden shaft 1.5 metres (5 feet) long and a pointed iron head of 0.6 metres (2 feet). This head was cleverly constructed. The first 25 centimetres (10 inches) were finely tempered to give it penetrating power, but the rest was left untempered so that it was fairly soft and liable to bend. Thus when the javelin was hurled at an enemy, from a distance of 23–28 metres (25–30 yards), its point penetrated and stuck into his shield, while the neck of the metal head bent and the shaft hung down. This not only made the javelin unusable, so that it could not be thrown back, but also made the encumbered shield so difficult to manage that the enemy might have to abandon it altogether.

When he had reached proficiency in handling his weapons and was physically fit, the soldier was ready to leave the barracks for training in the open countryside. This began with route marches on which he carried not only his body armour and weapons but also several days' ration of food, together with equipment for making an overnight camp, such as a saw, an axe and also a basket for moving earth, as shown in the picture below. Much importance was attached to the proper construction of the camp at the end of the day's march, and the young soldier was given careful instruction and practice. Several practice camps and forts have been found in Britain. For example, at Cawthorn in Yorkshire the soldiers under training did rather more than just dig ditches and ramparts; they also constructed platforms for catapults (ballistae) and even built camp ovens.

Relief from Trajan's column showing soldiers building a fort

Work

The fully trained legionary did not spend all or even much of his time on active service. Most of it was spent on peacetime duties, such as building or roadmaking, and, during the first century A.D. at least, he had good prospects of surviving till his discharge. He was generally stationed in a large legionary fortress somewhere near the frontiers of the empire in places such as Deva (Chester), Bonna (Bonn) and Vindobona (Vienna) which were key points in the Roman defences against the barbarians.

Many of the daily duties were the same wherever he was stationed. A duty roster, written on papyrus, has come down to us and lists the names of thirty-six soldiers, all members of the same century in one of the legions stationed in Egypt. It covers the first ten days in October possibly in the year A.D. 87. A selection of the entries is given on page 95 below. For example, C. Julius Valens was to spend October 2nd on guard duty in the tower of the fortress, October 4th repairing boots and October 8th acting as orderly (servant) to one of the officers.

Pay

In both war and peacetime the soldier received the same rate of pay. In the first century A.D., up to the time of the Emperor Domitian (A.D. 81–96), this amounted to 225 denarii per annum; Domitian improved the rate to 300 denarii. These amounts were gross pay, and before any money was handed to the soldier certain deductions were made. Surprising though it may seem, he was obliged to pay for his food, clothing and equipment. He would also leave some money in the military savings bank. What he actually received in cash may have been only a quarter or a fifth of his gross pay. Whether he felt badly treated is difficult to say. Certainly we know of cases of discontent, but pay and conditions of service were apparently not bad enough to discourage recruits. The soldier could look forward to some promotion and eventually an honourable discharge with a gratuity of 3,000 denarii or an allocation of land.

Promotion

If a soldier was promoted his life began to change in several ways. He was paid more and he was exempted from many of the fatigues performed by the ordinary soldier. Each century was commanded by a centurion and he was assisted by an optio who was waiting for a vacancy in the ranks of the centurions. There was also in each century a standard-bearer (signifer), a 'tesserārius' who commanded the guard-pickets and one or two clerks. The centurions, who were roughly equivalent to non-commissioned warrant officers in a modern army, were the backbone of the legion. There were sixty of them, each responsible for the training and discipline of a century, and their importance was reflected in their pay, which was probably about 1,500 denarii per annum. Most of them had risen from the ranks by virtue of courage and ability. The senior centurion of the legion (prīmus pīlus) was a highly respected figure; he was at least fifty years old and had worked his way up through the various grades of centurion. He held office for one year, then received a large gratuity and was allowed to retire; or he might go on still further to become 'praefectus castrōrum' (commander of the camp).

Senior officers

The men mentioned so far would expect to spend the whole of their working lives serving as professional soldiers. The senior officers, on the other hand, spent a much shorter period of time in the legion, possibly three or four years, without any previous service as centurion or ordinary legionary.

The officer commanding the legion was called a 'lēgātus'. He was a member of the Senate in Rome and usually fairly young, in his middle thirties. He was assisted by six military tribunes. Of these, one was usually a young man of noble birth, serving his military apprenticeship before starting a political career. The other five were members of a slightly lower social class (equitēs) and they too would be in their thirties. They were generally able, wealthy and educated men, often aiming at important posts in the imperial civil service.

	1 Oct.	2 Oct.	3 Oct.	4 Oct.	5 Oct.	6 Oct.	7 Oct.	8 Oct.	9 Oct.	10 Oct.
C. Julius Valens	training arena	tower	drainage	boots	armoury	armoury	baths	orderly	in century	baths
L. Sextilius Germanus	gate guard	standards	baths	tower	← duty in D. Decrius' century →					
M. Antonius Crispus	baths	stretchers in century	in century	plain clothes	in century	—	← tribune's escort →			
T. Flavius	—	—	—	baths	baths	baths	gate guard	—	—	—
M. Domitius	—	—	← detachment to the granaries at Neapolis →							

Words and phrases checklist

accidō, accidere, accidī – happen
aliquis – someone
aperiō, aperīre, aperuī, apertus – open
autem – but
captīvus, captīvī – prisoner, captive
castra, castrōrum – camp
cōgō, cōgere, coēgī, coāctus – force, compel
dēpōnō, dēpōnere, dēposuī, dēpositus – put down, take off
dēsinō, dēsinere – end, cease
dignitās, dignitātis – importance, prestige
dīligentia, dīligentiae – industry, hard work
explicō, explicāre, explicāvī, explicātus – explain
extrā – outside
furēns, *gen.* furentis – furious, in a rage
haesitō, haesitāre, haesitāvī – hesitate
immemor, *gen.* immemoris – forgetful
immortālis, immortāle – immortal
  dī immortālēs! – heavens above!
laedō, laedere, laesī, laesus – harm
lateō, latēre, latuī – lie hidden
legiō, legiōnis – legion
nescio, nescīre, nescīvī – not know
nōmen, nōminis – name
ōs, ōris – face
poena, poenae – punishment
  poenās dare – pay the penalty, be punished
rūrsus – again
scelestus, scelesta, scelestum – wicked
statiō, statiōnis – post
suāvis, suāve – sweet
testis, testis – witness

Agricola

adventus Agricolae

mīlitēs legiōnis secundae, quī Dēvae in castrīs erant, diū et strēnuē labōrābant. nam Gāius Iūlius Sīlānus, lēgātus legiōnis, adventum Agricolae exspectābat. mīlitēs, ā centuriōnibus iussī, multa et varia faciēbant. aliī arma poliēbant; aliī aedificia pūrgābant; aliī plaustra reficiēbant. Sīlānus neque quiētem neque commeātum mīlitibus 5 dedit.

mīlitēs, ignārī adventūs Agricolae, rem graviter ferēbant. trēs continuōs diēs labōrāvērunt; quārtō diē Sīlānus adventum Agricolae nūntiāvit. mīlitēs, cum hoc audīvissent, maximē gaudēbant quod Agricolam dīligēbant. 10

tertiā hōrā Sīlānus mīlitēs in ōrdinēs longōs īnstrūxit, ut Agricolam salūtārent. mīlitēs, cum Agricolam castra intrantem vīdissent, magnum clāmōrem sustulērunt.

'iō, Agricola! iō, iō, Agricola!'

Agricola ad tribūnal prōcessit ut pauca dīceret. omnēs statim 15 tacuērunt ut contiōnem Agricolae audīrent.

'gaudeō', inquit, 'quod hodiē vōs rūrsus videō. nūllam legiōnem fidēliōrem habeō, nūllam fortiōrem. disciplīnam studiumque vestrum valdē laudō.'

mīlitēs ita hortātus, per ōrdinēs prōcessit ut eōs īnspiceret. deinde 20 prīncipia intrāvit ut colloquium cum Sīlānō habēret.

adventus *arrival*	quārtō diē *on the fourth day*
Dēvae *at Chester*	gaudēbant: gaudēre *be pleased, rejoice*
strēnuē *hard, energetically*	tertiā hōrā *at the third hour*
aliī . . . aliī . . . aliī *some . . . others*	iō! *hurray!*
. . . *others*	tribūnal *platform*
arma *arms, weapons*	contiōnem: contiō *speech*
poliēbant: polīre *polish*	disciplīnam: disciplīna *discipline,*
pūrgābant: pūrgāre *clean*	*orderliness*
quiētem: quiēs *rest*	studium *enthusiasm, keenness*
commeātum: commeātus *leave*	vestrum: vester *your*
trēs . . . diēs *for three days*	hortātus *having encouraged*
continuōs: continuus *continuous, on end*	prīncipia *headquarters*

When you have read this story, answer the questions at the end.

in prīncipiīs

Salvius ipse paulō prius ad castra advēnerat. iam in legiōnis
secundae prīncipiīs sedēbat, Agricolam anxius exspectāns.
sollicitus erat quod in epistulā, quam ad Agricolam mīserat, multa
falsa scrīpserat. in prīmīs Cogidubnum sēditiōnis accūsāverat. in
animō volvēbat num Agricola sibi crēditūrus esset. Belimicum 5
sēcum dūxerat ut testis esset.

subitō Salvius, Agricolam intrantem cōnspicātus, ad eum
festīnāvit ut salūtāret. deinde renovāvit ea quae in epistulā
scrīpserat. Agricola, cum haec audīvisset, diū tacuit. dēnique
maximē commōtus, 10

'quanta perfidia!' inquit. 'quanta īnsānia! id quod mihi
patefēcistī, vix intellegere possum. īnsānīvit Cogidubnus.
īnsānīvērunt prīncipēs Rēgnēnsium. numquam nōs oportet
barbarīs crēdere; tūtius est eōs omnēs prō hostibus habēre. nunc
mihi necesse est rēgem opprimere quem quīnque annōs prō amīcō 15
habeō.'

haec locūtus, ad Sīlānum, lēgātum legiōnis, sē vertit.

'Sīlāne', inquit, 'nōs oportet rēgem prīncipēsque Rēgnēnsium
quam celerrimē opprimere. tibī statim cum duābus cohortibus
prōficīscendum est.' 20

Sīlānus, ē prīncipiīs ēgressus, centuriōnibus mandāta dedit. eōs
iussit cohortēs parāre. intereā Agricola plūra dē rēgis perfidiā
rogāre coepit. Salvius eī respondit,

paulō prius *a little earlier*
in prīmīs *in particular*
sēditiōnis: sēditiō *rebellion*
in animō volvēbat: in animō volvere
  wonder, turn over in the mind
num *whether*
crēditūrus *going to believe*
renovāvit: renovāre *repeat, renew*

īnsānia *madness, insanity*
nōs oportet *we must*
prō hostibus habēre *reckon as enemies*
opprimere *crush*
tibi . . . prōficīscendum est *you must
  set out*
cohortibus: cohors *cohort*

'ecce Belimicus, vir ingeniī optimī summaeque fideī, quem iste
Cogidubnus corrumpere temptābat. Belimicus autem, quī 25
blanditiās rēgis spernēbat, omnia mihi patefēcit.'

'id quod Salvius dīxit vērum est', inquit Belimicus. 'rēx Rōmānōs
ōdit. Rōmānōs ē Britanniā expellere tōtamque īnsulam occupāre
cupit. nāvēs igitur comparat. mīlitēs exercet. etiam bēstiās saevās
colligit. nūper bēstiam in mē impulit ut mē interficeret.'   30

Agricola tamen hīs verbīs diffīsus, Salvium dīligentius rogāvit
quae indicia sēditiōnis vīdisset. cognōscere voluit quot essent
armātī, num Britannī cīvēs Rōmānōs interfēcissent, quās urbēs
dēlēvissent.

subitō magnum clāmōrem omnēs audīvērunt. per iānuam 35
prīncipiōrum perrūpit homō squālidus. ad Agricolam praeceps
cucurrit genibusque eius haesit.

'cīvis Rōmānus sum', inquit. 'Quīntum Caecilium Iūcundum mē
vocant. ego multās iniūriās passus hūc tandem advēnī. hoc ūnum
dīcere volō. Cogidubnus est innocēns.'   40

haec locūtus humī prōcubuit exanimātus.

corrumpere *corrupt*
blanditiās: blanditiae *flatteries*
spernēbat: spernere *despise, reject*
diffīsus *having distrusted*
indicia: indicium *sign, evidence*
armātī: armātus *armed*
perrūpit: perrumpere *burst through, burst in*
squālidus *covered in dirt, filthy*

1 Why has Salvius come to Chester?
2 Why has he brought Belimicus with him?
3 Why do you think Agricola stays silent for a long time (line 9)?
4 What orders does he give to Silanus?
5 Why does Agricola feel doubtful about Belimicus' statement?
6 What questions does Agricola put to Salvius? Would Salvius find
   Agricola's questions easy to answer? Do you think Agricola ought
   to have asked these questions *before* sending out the cohorts?
7 What happens before Salvius can answer Agricola?
8 What is the first thing Quintus says? Why does he say this first?

About the language

1   Study the following examples:

mīlitēs ad prīncipia convēnērunt **ut Agricolam audīrent**.
The soldiers gathered at the headquarters in order that they might hear Agricola.

per tōtam noctem labōrābat medicus **ut vulnera mīlitum sānāret**.
The doctor worked all night in order that he might treat the soldiers' wounds.

The groups of words in heavy print are known as *purpose clauses*, because they indicate the *purpose* for which an action was done. For instance, in the second example above, the group of words 'ut vulnera mīlitum sānāret' indicates the purpose of the doctor's work. The verb in a purpose clause in Latin is always subjunctive.

2   Further examples:

1   dominus stilum et cērās poposcit ut epistulam scrīberet.
2   omnēs cīvēs ad silvam contendērunt ut leōnem mortuum spectārent.
3   dēnique ego ad patrem rediī ut rem explicārem.
4   pugiōnem rapuī ut captīvum interficerem.

3   Instead of translating 'ut' and the subjunctive as 'in order that he (they) might . . .', it is often possible to use a simpler form of words:

mīlitēs ad prīncipia convēnērunt ut Agricolam audīrent.
The soldiers gathered at the headquarters in order to hear Agricola.
   or, simpler still:
The soldiers gathered at the headquarters to hear Agricola.

tribūnus

Agricola, ubi hoc vīdit, custōdēs iussit Quīntum auferre medicumque arcessere. tum ad tribūnum mīlitum, quī adstābat, sē vertit.

'mī Rūfe', inquit, 'prūdentissimus es omnium tribūnōrum quōs habeō. tē iubeō hunc hominem summā cum cūrā interrogāre.' 5

Salvius, cum Rūfus exiisset, valdē commōtus,

'cūr tempus terimus?' inquit. 'omnia explicāre possum. nōtus est mihi hic homō. nūper in vīllā mē vīsitāvit, quamquam nōn invītāveram. trēs mēnsēs apud mē mānsit, opēs meās dēvorāns. duōs tripodas argenteōs habēbam, quōs abstulit ut Cogidubnō 10 daret. sed eum nōn accūsāvī, quod hospes erat. ubi tamen Aquās Sūlis mēcum advēnit, facinus scelestum committere temptāvit. venēnum parāvit ut Memorem, haruspicem Rōmānum, necāret. postquam rem nōn effēcit, mē ipsum accūsāvit. nōlī eī crēdere.

multō perfidior est quam Britannī.'   15
    haec cum audīvisset, Agricola respondit,
    'sī tālia fēcit, eī moriendum est.'
    mox revēnit Rūfus valdē attonitus.
    'Quīntus Caecilius', inquit, 'est iuvenis summae fideī. patrem
meum, quem Alexandrīae relīquī, bene nōverat. hoc prō certō 20
habeō quod Quīntus hanc epistulam mihi ostendit, ā patre ipsō
scrīptam.'
    Agricola statim Quīntum ad sē vocāvit, cēterōsque dīmīsit.
Salvius, Quīntum dētestātus, anxius exiit. Agricola cum Quīntō
colloquium trēs hōrās habēbat.   25

tribūnus *tribune (high-ranking officer)*
prūdentissimus: prūdēns *shrewd,*
    intelligent
tempus terimus: tempus terere *waste*
    time
opēs *money, wealth*

dēvorāns: dēvorāre *devour, eat up*
multō perfidior *much more treacherous*
tālia *such things*
prō certō habeō: prō certō habēre
    know for certain
dētestātus *having cursed*

About the language

1   From Stage 14 onwards you have met sentences of this kind:

    necesse est mihi cēnam parāre.   I must prepare the dinner.
    necesse est vōbīs labōrāre.   You must work.

2   You have now met another way of expressing the same idea:

    necesse est nōbīs currere. }
    nōbīs **currendum** est.   }   We must run.

    necesse est eī revenīre.   }
    eī **reveniendum** est.   }   He must come back.

    The word in heavy print is known as the *gerundive*.

3   Further examples:

    1 mihi fugiendum est.
    2 nōbīs ambulandum est.
    3 tibi hīc manendum est.
    4 omnibus servīs labōrandum est.

contentiō

Agricola, cum Quīntum audīvisset, vehementer saeviēbat. Salvium furēns arcessīvit. quī, simulatque intrāvit, aliquid dīcere coepit. Agricola tamen, cum silentium iussisset, Salvium vehementer accūsāvit.

'dī immortālēs! Cogidubnus est innocēns, tū perfidus. cūr tam 5 īnsānus eram ut tibi crēderem? quīnque annōs hanc prōvinciam iam administrō. rēgem Cogidubnum bene cognōvī. saepe rēx mihi auxiliō fuit. neque perfidum neque mendācem umquam sē praestitit. cūr tū crīmen falsum in eum intulistī? accūsāvistīne eum ut potentiam tuam augērēs? simulatque ad hanc prōvinciam 10 vēnistī, amīcī mē dē calliditāte tuā monuērunt. nunc rēs ipsa mē docuit. num Imperātor Domitiānus hanc tantam perfidiam ferre potest? ego sānē nōn possum. in hāc prōvinciā summam potestātem habeō. iubeō tē hās inimīcitiās dēpōnere. iubeō tē ad Cogidubnī aulam īre, veniamque ab eō petere. praetereā tē oportet Imperātōrī ipsī rem explicāre.'

haec ubi dīxit Agricola, Salvius respondit īrātus,

'quam caecus es! quam longē errās! tē ipsum oportet Imperātōrī id quod in Britanniā fēcistī explicāre. quīnque annōs hanc prōvinciam pessimē administrās. tū enim in ultimīs Britanniae partibus bellum geris et victōriās inānēs ē Calēdoniā refers; sed Imperātor pecūniās opēsque accipere cupit. itaque rēgnum Cogidubnī occupāre cōnstituit; Calēdoniam floccī nōn facit. tū sānē hoc nescīs. in magnō perīculō es, quod cōnsilium meum spernis. nōn sōlum mihi sed Imperātōrī ipsī obstās.'

cum hanc contentiōnem inter sē habērent, subitō nūntius prīncipia ingressus exclāmāvit,

'mortuus est Cogidubnus!'

auxiliō fuit *was a help, was helpful*
potentiam: potentia *power*
augērēs: augēre *increase*
inimīcitiās: inimīcitia *feud, quarrel*
tē oportet *you must*
caecus *blind*
pessimē *very badly*
victōriās: victōria *victory*
inānēs: inānis *empty, meaningless*
Calēdoniā: Calēdonia *Scotland*
cōnstituit: cōnstituere *decide*

Practising the language

1 Study the form and meaning of the following verbs and nouns, and give the meaning of the untranslated words:

amāre	to love	amor	love
timēre	to be afraid	timor	fear
honōrāre	to honour	honor	
clāmāre		clāmor	
labōrāre		labor	
fulgēre		fulgor	brightness
pavēre	to be alarmed	pavor	
furere		furor	madness, fury
tremere		tremor	a shaking, a tremor
dolēre (1)	to hurt, to be painful	dolor (1)	
dolēre (2)	to be sad	dolor (2)	

Give the meaning of the following nouns:

favor, pallor, sūdor

2 Complete each sentence with the right word and then translate.

1 Agricola, ubi verba . . . . . audīvit, Salvium arcessīvit. (Quīntum, Quīntī, Quīntō)

2 omnēs hospitēs . . . . . saltātrīcis laudāvērunt. (artem, artis, artī)

3 iter nostrum difficile erat, quod tot cīvēs . . . . . complēbant. (viās, viārum, viīs)

4 prō prīncipiīs stābat magna turba . . . . . . (mīlitēs, mīlitum, mīlitibus)

5 lēgātus, postquam mandāta . . . . . dedit, legiōnem ad montem proximum dūxit. (centuriōnēs, centuriōnum, centuriōnibus)

6 iūdex, quī . . . . . nōn crēdēbat, īrātissimus fīēbat. (puerōs, puerōrum, puerīs)

3 Translate each English sentence into Latin by selecting correctly from the list of Latin words.

1 The kind citizens had provided help.
    cīvis   benignī   auxilium   praebuērunt
    cīvēs   benignōs   auxiliī   praebuerant

2 They arrested the soldier in the kitchen of an inn.
    mīlitem   per culīnam   tabernae   comprehendunt
    mīlitis   in culīnā   tabernārum   comprehendērunt

3 Master! Read this letter!
    domine   haec   epistula   lege
    dominus   hanc   epistulam   legis

4 The old men departed, praising the brave messenger.
    senēs   discēdunt   fortem   nūntium   laudāns
    senum   discessērunt   fortī   nūntiōs   laudantēs

5 How can we avoid the punishments of the gods?
    quō modō   poenae   deōrum   vītantēs   possumus
    quis   poenās   deīs   vītāre   poterāmus

6 The words of the soothsayer frightened him.
    verbum   haruspicis   eam   eum   terruit
    verba   haruspicī   eōs   terruērunt

4 Complete each sentence with the most suitable word from the list below, and then translate.

epistulam, audīvisset, ēgressus, invēnērunt, equīs, captī

1 Salvius, ē prīncipiīs . . . . ., Belimicum quaesīvit.
2 Agricola, cum haec verba . . . . ., ad Rūfum sē vertit.
3 dominus . . . . . ē manibus servī impatiēns rapuit.
4 custōdēs nūntium humī iacentem . . . . . .
5 quattuor Britannī, in pugnā . . . . ., vītam miserrimam in carcere agēbant.
6 aliī mīlitēs . . . . . aquam dabant, aliī frūmentum in horrea īnferēbant.

Agricola, governor of Britain

With the abbreviated words written out, this reads:
imperatore Vespasiano VIIII Tito imperatore VII consule Cnaeo
Iulio Agricola legato Augusti propraetore.

The two inscriptions above both contain the name of Gnaeus Julius
Agricola. The first comes from a lead water-pipe found at Chester,
the second from the forum of Verulamium (St Albans). These
inscriptions might have been virtually all that we knew about the
man if his life-story had not been written by his son-in-law, the
historian Tacitus. Because of Tacitus' biography we possess a very
detailed picture of Agricola.

He was born on June 13, A.D. 40 in the Roman colony of Forum
Iulii in south-east Gaul. The town had been founded by Julius
Caesar for his veteran soldiers, and most of its inhabitants were
Italian-born citizens rather than native Gauls. (It is today the
French town of Fréjus.) He came from a distinguished family. His
grandfathers had both held important government posts and his
father had been made a senator by the Emperor Tiberius, but later
fell foul of the Emperor Gaius Caligula and was executed in A.D. 40,
shortly after Agricola was born.

Agricola went to school at Massilia (Marseilles), which was the
cultural and educational centre of southern Gaul. He followed the
normal curriculum for the young sons of upper-class Roman

families: public speaking (taught by a 'rhētor') and philosophy. He enjoyed the latter, but Tacitus records his mother's reaction:

'I remember that Agricola often told us that in his youth he was more enthusiastic about philosophy than a Roman and a senator was expected to be, and his mother thought it wise to put a damper on such a passionate interest.'

At the age of eighteen, Agricola served in the Roman army in Britain with the rank of 'tribūnus', like Barbillus Rufus in the story on p. 102. He used this opportunity to become familiar with the province. The soldiers under his command had a similar opportunity to get to know him. Two years later, during the revolt of Boudica in A.D. 60, he witnessed the grim realities of warfare. Agricola was by now very knowledgeable about the province of Britain and this knowledge was to stand him in good stead during his governorship some eighteen years later.

Back in Rome, he continued his political career. In A.D. 70, he returned to Britain to take command of the Twentieth Legion which was stationed at Viroconium (Wroxeter) and had become undisciplined and troublesome. His success in handling this difficult task was rewarded by promotion to the governorship of Aquitania in Gaul. In A.D. 77 he became consul and the following year returned to Britain for a third time, as governor of the province. The political experience and military skill which he had acquired by then equipped him to face an exciting, if demanding, situation.

Agricola rose to the challenge in many different ways. He actively promoted a policy of romanisation; he extended a network of roads and forts across northern Britain, including the legionary fortress at Chester; and during his governorship he virtually doubled the area of Roman-held territory in Britain.

Career of Agricola

A.D.		
58	Tribunus Militum in Britain
64	Quaestor in Asia
66	Tribunus Plebis in Rome
68	Praetor in Rome
70	Commander of Twentieth Legion in Britain
74	Governor of Aquitania
77	Consul
78	Governor of Britain

Words and phrases checklist

accūsō, accūsāre, accūsāvī, accūsātus – accuse
auferō, auferre, abstulī, ablātus – take away, steal
bellum, bellī – war
   bellum gerere – wage war, campaign
cohors, cohortis – cohort
colligō, colligere, collēgī, collēctus – gather, collect
commōtus, commōta, commōtum – moved, excited, upset
doceō, docēre, docuī, doctus – teach
facinus, facinoris – crime
falsus, falsa, falsum – false, dishonest
fidēs, fideī – loyalty, trustworthiness
īnsānus, īnsāna, īnsānum – mad, crazy, insane
īnstruō, īnstruere, īnstrūxī, īnstrūctus – draw up
lēgātus, lēgātī – commander
num – whether
occupō, occupāre, occupāvī, occupātus – seize, take over
oportet – it is right
   mē oportet – I must
perfidia, perfidiae – treachery
praebeō, praebēre, praebuī, praebitus – provide
prīncipia, prīncipiōrum – headquarters
prōvincia, prōvinciae – province
quot? – how many?
referō, referre, rettulī, relātus – bring back
rēgnum, rēgnī – kingdom
saevus, saeva, saevum – savage, cruel
sānē – obviously
sī – if
tribūnus, tribūnī – tribune (high-ranking officer)
ultimus, ultima, ultimum – furthest
ut – that, in order that

in castrīs

'fuge mēcum ad horreum!'

Go and get the men ready to set with the 'Centurion

extrā carcerem, Modestus et Strȳthiō sermōnem anxiī habēbant.
Modestus Strȳthiōnem monēbat ut ad horreum sēcum fugeret.

Sent an menk strypoff

'invenīte Modestum Strȳthiōnemque!'

Go

prō prīncipiīs, centuriō Valerius mīlitibus mandāta dabat.
centuriō mīlitibus imperābat ut Modestum Strȳthiōnemque invenīrent.

The romans are taking our men, lets get them.

'castra Rōmāna oppugnāte!
horrea incendite!'

in silvā proximā, Vercobrix contiōnem apud Britannōs habēbat.
Vercobrix Britannōs incitābat ut castra Rōmāna oppugnārent et horrea incenderent.

When you have read this story, answer the questions at the end.

sub horreō

Modestus et Strȳthiō, ē carcere ēgressī, ad horreum fūgērunt. per aditum angustum rēpsērunt et sub horreō cēlātī manēbant. centuriō Valerius, cum portās cellārum apertās carceremque dēsertum vīdisset, īrātissimus erat. mīlitibus imperāvit ut Modestum et Strȳthiōnem caperent. mīlitēs tamen, quamquam per tōta castra 5 quaerēbant, eōs invenīre nōn poterant. illī quīnque diēs mānsērunt cēlātī. sextō diē Modestus tam miser erat ut rem diūtius ferre nōn posset.

Modestus: quam īnfēlīx sum! mālim in illō carcere esse potius quam sub hōc horreō latēre. quālis est haec vīta? 10 necesse est mihi grāna quae mūrēs relīquērunt cōnsūmere. adest Strȳthiō, comes exiliī, sed mē nōn adiuvat. nam Strȳthiō est vir maximī silentiī, minimīque iocī. ēheu! mē taedet huius vītae.

Strȳthiō: mī Modeste, difficile est nōbīs sub horreō diūtius 15 manēre. nunc tamen advesperāscit. vīsne mē, ex horreō ēgressum, cibum quaerere? hominibus miserrimīs cibus sōlācium semper affert.

Modestus: id est cōnsilium optimum. nōbīs cēnandum est. Strȳthiō, tē huic reī praeficiō. ī prīmum ad coquum. 20 eum iubē cēnam splendidam coquere et hūc portāre. deinde quaere Aulum et Pūblicum, amīcōs nostrōs!

aditum: aditus *entrance*
angustum: angustus *narrow*
rēpsērunt: rēpere *crawl*
imperāvit: imperāre *order, command*
sextō: sextus *sixth*
mālim *I should prefer*
potius *rather*
grāna: grānum *grain*

exiliī: exilium *exile*
mē taedet *I am tired, I am bored*
advesperāscit: advesperāscere *get dark, become dark*
sōlācium *comfort*
affert: afferre *bring*
praeficiō: praeficere *put in charge*
prīmum *first*

invītā eōs ad cēnam! iubē Aulum amphoram vīnī ferre,
Pūblicum lucernam āleāsque. tum curre ad vīcum;
Nigrīnam quaere! optima est saltātrīcum; mihi 25
saltātrīcēs quoque sōlācium afferunt.

Strȳthiō: quid dīcis? vīsne mē saltātrīcem in castra dūcere?

Modestus: abī caudex!

Strȳthiō, ut mandāta Modestī efficeret, invītus discessit. coquō
persuāsit ut cēnam splendidam parāret; Aulō et Pūblicō persuāsit 30
ut vīnum et lucernam āleāsque ferrent; Nigrīnam ōrāvit ut ad
horreum venīret, sed eī persuādēre nōn poterat.

vīcum: vīcus *town, village*
ōrāvit: ōrāre *beg*

1 What was the purpose of a 'horreum'? Why was its floor raised
above ground level? What does this enable Modestus and
Strythio to do?
2 After five days, what has Modestus been forced to do?
3 What makes Strythio think he can go outside without getting
caught?
4 Who is to bring the dinner to the granary? What are Aulus and
Publicus to bring? Who else is to come to the dinner? Where is she
to be found?
5 Why is Strythio 'invītus' (line 29)? How successful is he in
carrying out Modestus' instructions?
6 Which would you expect to be built first, the 'castra' or the
'vīcus'?

About the language

1 In Unit I, you met sentences like this:

'redīte!'   'pecūniam trāde!'
'Go back!'   'Hand over the money!'

In each example, an order or command is being *given*. These
examples are known as *direct* commands.

2 In Stage 27, you have met sentences like this:

lēgātus mīlitibus imperāvit ut redīrent.
The commander ordered his soldiers that they should go back.
   or, in more natural English:
The commander ordered his soldiers to go back.

latrōnēs mercātōrī imperāvērunt ut pecūniam trāderet.
The robbers ordered the merchant that he should hand over the
money.
   or, in more natural English:
The robbers ordered the merchant to hand over the money.

In each of these examples, the command is not being given, but
is being *reported* or *mentioned*. These examples are known as
indirect commands. The verb in an indirect command in Latin is
usually subjunctive.

3 Compare the following examples:

direct commands	*indirect commands*
'contendite!'	iuvenis amīcīs persuāsit ut contenderent.
'Hurry!'	The young man persuaded his friends to hurry.
'dā mihi aquam!'	captīvus custōdem ōrāvit ut aquam sibi daret.
'Give me water!'	The prisoner begged the guard to give him water.
'fuge!'	mē monuit ut fugerem.
'Run away!'	He warned me to run away.

4 Further examples of direct and indirect commands:

1 nēmō ancillae persuādēre poterat ut saltāret.
2 'tacē!'
3 centuriō mihi imperāvit ut tacērem.
4 vōs saepe monēbam ut dīligenter labōrārētis.
5 'parcite mihi!'
6 senex nōs ōrābat ut sibi parcerēmus.
7 coquus servīs imperāvit ut vīnum in mēnsam pōnerent.
8 comitēs mercātōrem monuērunt ut ab oppidō clam discēderet.

Modestus prōmōtus

cum Strȳthiō cēnam et amīcōs quaereret, decem Britannī ā Vercobrige ductī, castrīs cautē appropinquābant. Vercobrix enim eīs persuāserat ut castra oppugnārent. Britannī, postquam custōdēs vītāvērunt, vallum tacitē trānscendērunt et castra intrāvērunt. in manibus facēs tenēbant ut horrea incenderent. celeriter ad horrea 5 advēnērunt quod prius cognōverant ubi sita essent.

Modestus, ignārus adventūs Britannōrum, sub horreō sedēbat. adeō ēsuriēbat ut dē vītā paene dēspērāret. per parvam rīmam prōspiciēbat, reditum Strȳthiōnis exspectāns.

'trēs hōrās Strȳthiōnem iam exspectō. quid eī accidit?'   1
subitō manum hominum per tenebrās cōnspexit.
'euge! tandem vēnērunt amīcī! heus, amīcī, hūc venīte!'

Britannī, cum Modestī vōcem audīvissent, erant tam attonitī, ut immōtī stārent. respondēre nōn audēbant. Vercobrix tamen, quī raucam Modestī vōcem agnōverat, ad comitēs versus,

'nōlīte timēre', inquit susurrāns. 'nōtus est mihi hic mīles. stultior est quam asinus. nōbīs nocēre nōn potest.'

tum Britannī per aditum tacitī rēpsērunt. simulatque intrāvērunt, Modestus eīs obviam iit, ut salūtāret.

'salvēte, amīcī! nunc nōbīs cēnandum ac bibendum est.'

tum Britannus quīdam, vir ingēns, in Modestum incurrit.

'ō Nigrīna, dēliciae meae!' clāmāvit Modestus. 'tē nōn agnōvī! quam longī sunt capillī tuī! age! cōnsīde prope mē! dā mihi ōsculum! quis lucernam habet?'

Vercobrix, cum Modestum lucernam rogantem audīvisset, Britannīs imperāvit ut facēs incenderent. Modestus, Vercobrigem Britannōsque cōnspicātus, palluit.

'dī immortālēs!' inquit. 'abiit Nigrīna, appāruērunt Britannī! mihi statim effugiendum est.'

Vercobrix tamen suīs imperāvit ut Modestum comprehenderent. ūnus ē Britannīs Modestō appropinquāvit ut dēligāret. fax, tamen, quam tenēbat, tunicam Modestī forte incendit.

'ēheu!' ululāvit ille. 'ardeō! mē dēvorant flammae!'

tum ē manibus Britannōrum ēlāpsus fūgit praeceps. simulac per
aditum ērūpit, Strȳthiōnī amīcīsque occurrit. amphoram vīnī ē 35
manibus Aulī ēripuit et vīnum in tunicam fūdit.

'īnsānit Modestus!' clāmāvit Strȳthiō attonitus.

Modestus tamen, Strȳthiōnis clāmōrum neglegēns, amphoram in
aditum impulit. tum in amphoram innīxus, magnōs clāmōrēs
sustulit.   40

'subvenīte! subvenīte! Britannōs cēpī!'

statim manus mīlitum, ā Valeriō ducta, ad horrea contendit.

prōmōtus: prōmovēre *promote*	obviam iit: obviam īre *meet, go to meet*
vallum *rampart*	incurrit: incurrere *bump into*
trānscendērunt: trānscendere *climb over*	suīs: suī *his men*
facēs: fax *torch*	ēripuit: ēripere *snatch, tear*
rīmam: rīma *crack, chink*	innīxus *having leant*
prōspiciēbat: prōspicere *look out*	subvenīte: subvenīre *help, come to help*
versus *having turned*	

117

tantī erant clāmōrēs Modestī ut tōta castra complērent. praefectus castrōrum ipse accurrit ut causam strepitūs cognōsceret.

Modestus exsultāns 'īnsidiās Britannīs parāvī', inquit. 45 'Vercobrix ipse multīs cum Britannīs sub horreō inclūsus est.'

breve erat certāmen. tantus erat numerus mīlitum Rōmānōrum ut Britannōs facile superārent. Rōmānī Britannōs ex horreō extractōs ad carcerem redūxērunt. tum lēgātus legiōnis ipse Modestum arcessītum laudāvit. 50

'Modeste', inquit, 'mīlitem fortiōrem quam tē numquam anteā vīdī. sōlus decem hostibus īnsidiās parāvistī. nōs decet praemium tibi dare.'

Modestus, ā lēgātō ita laudātus, adeō gaudēbat ut vix sē continēre posset. pecūniam laetus exspectābat. 55

'carcerī tē praeficiō', inquit lēgātus.

praefectus *commander*
causam: causa *reason, cause*
strepitūs: strepitus *noise, din*
breve: brevis *short, brief*

certāmen *struggle, fight*
redūxērunt: redūcere *lead back*
nōs decet *it is proper for us*
continēre *contain*

Antefix bearing name and emblem of the Twentieth Legion who were stationed at Chester after A.D.87

About the language

1   In Stage 11, you met the verb 'placet'. Notice again how it is used:

mihi placet hoc dōnum accipere.
It pleases me to receive this present.
   or, in more natural English:
I am glad to receive this present.

nōbīs placet.
It pleases us.
   or, in more natural English:
We like it.

2   The following verbs are used in a similar way:

nōs **decet** praemium Modestō dare.
It is proper for us to give a reward to Modestus.
   or, more naturally:
We ought to give a reward to Modestus.

mē **taedet** huius vītae.
It makes me tired of this life.
   or, more naturally:
I am tired of this life.

Rōmānōs numquam **oportet** hostibus crēdere.
It is never right for Romans to trust the enemy.
   or, more naturally:
Romans must never trust the enemy.

3   These verbs are known as *impersonal* verbs.

4   Further examples:

  1 tibi placet?
  2 saltātrīcem spectāre volō! mē taedet cibī et vīnī!
  3 semper pluit!
  4 Britannōs decet extrā aulam manēre.
  5 nunc advesperāscit.
  6 nōs oportet rēgnum Cogidubnī occupāre.

Practising the language

1 Study the form and meaning of the following adjectives and nouns, and give the meaning of the untranslated words:

altus	high, deep	altitūdō	height, depth
magnus	big	magnitūdō	size
pulcher	beautiful	pulchritūdō	
sollicitus		sollicitūdō	
lātus	wide	lātitūdō	
mānsuētus	tame	mānsuētūdō	
sōlus		sōlitūdō	

Give the meaning of the following nouns:

fortitūdō, longitūdō, multitūdō

Notice some slightly different examples:

cupere	to desire	cupīdō	a desire
		Cupīdō	god of Love, god of Desire
valēre	to be well	valētūdō	health: (1) good health
			(2) bad health, illness

The imperative of 'valēre' has a special meaning which you have often met:

valē   be well, i.e. fare well, goodbye

2 Complete each sentence with the right word from the list below and then translate.

missōs, līberātī, territa, regressam, tenentēs, passus

1 captīvī, ē cellīs subitō . . . . ., ad portam carceris ruērunt.
2 Britannī, hastās in manibus . . . . ., in īnsidiīs latēbant.
3 ancilla, ā dominō īrātō . . . . ., respondēre nōn audēbat.
4 Cogidubnus, tot iniūriās . . . . ., omnēs Rōmānōs ōdit.
5 māter puellam, ē tabernā tandem . . . . ., vehementer vituperāvit.
6 centuriō mīlitēs, ex Italiā nūper ab imperātōre . . . . ., īnspexit.

3 Translate the following sentences, then change the words in heavy print from singular to plural, and translate again. You will sometimes need to look up the gender of a noun in the 'Words and phrases' section of the Language Information pamphlet, and you may need to refer to the table of nouns on pages 4–6 of that pamphlet, especially to check the endings of *neuter* nouns.

1 imperātor **īnsulam** vīsitābat.
2 **nauta** pecūniam **poscēbat**.
3 iuvenēs **captīvum** custōdiēbant.
4 fūr **pōculum** īnspiciēbat.
5 ōmina **haruspicem** terrēbant.
6 **plaustrum** in agrō **stābat**.

4 With the help of the table of nouns on pages 4–6 of the Language Information pamphlet, complete the sentences of this exercise with the right form of each unfinished word, and then translate.

1 servus prope iānuam stābat. serv. . . pecūniam dedimus.
2 puerī per viam currēbant. clāmōrēs puer. . . mē excitāvērunt.
3 puella tabernam meam intrāvit. puell. . . multās gemmās ostendī.
4 Salvius ad aulam rēg. . . quam celerrimē contendit.
5 Memor, ubi nōm. . . tuum audīvit, perterritus erat.
6 in hāc viā sunt duo templ. . . .
7 mercātor ad fundum meum herī vēnit. frūmentum meum mercātor. . . vēndidī.
8 magna multitūdō cīv. . . nōbīs obstābat.
9 barbarī prōvinciam oppugnāvērunt, multāsque urb. . . dēlēvērunt.
10 leōnēs saeviēbant; nam servus stultus nūllum cibum leō. . . dederat.
11 serv. . . dēnāriōs quōs tenēbam rapuērunt.
12 iūdex mercātor. . ., quī fēminam dēcēperat, pūnīvit.

About the language

1 Study the following examples:

tanta erat multitūdō **ut tōtam aulam complēret**.
So great was the crowd that it filled the whole palace.

iuvenis gemmās adeō cupiēbat **ut pecūniam statim trāderet**.
The young man wanted the jewels so much that he handed over
the money immediately.

The groups of words in heavy print are known as *result clauses*,
because they indicate a *result*. For instance, in the first example
above, the group of words 'ut tōtam aulam complēret' indicates
the result of the crowd's size. The verb in a result clause in Latin
is always subjunctive.

2 Further examples:

1 tam stultus erat puer ut omnēs eum dērīdērent.
2 tantus erat clāmor ut nēmō iussa centuriōnum audīret.
3 Agricola tot mīlitēs ēmīsit ut hostēs fugerent.
4 adeō saeviēbat Valerius ut sē continēre nōn posset.

The legionary fortress

If the legion itself was like an army in miniature, the fortress in
which it lived when not on campaign may be compared to a fortified
town. It covered about 20–25 hectares (50–60 acres), about one
third of the area of Pompeii. The design of the fortress was based on
a standard pattern, illustrated opposite.

The chief buildings, grouped in the centre, were the headquarters
(prīncipia), the living-quarters of the commanding officer
(praetōrium), the hospital (valētūdinārium), and the granaries
(horrea). Numerous streets and alleys criss-crossed the fortress, but
there were three main streets: the 'via praetōria' ran from the main
gate to the front entrance of the principia; the 'via prīncipālis'

extended across the whole width of the fortress, making a T-junction with the via praetoria just in front of the principia; the 'via quīntāna' passed behind the principia and extended across the width of the fortress. The fortress was surrounded by a ditch, rampart and battlements, with towers at the corners and at intervals along the sides. Each side had a fortified gateway.

Plan of a legionary fortress (based on Chester)

amphitheatre

The principia was the heart of the legion and was therefore a large, complex and impressive building. A visitor would first enter a stone-flagged courtyard surrounded on three sides by a colonnade and storerooms. On the far side of the courtyard was the great hall or basilica, where the commander worked with his officers, interviewed important local people and administered military justice. It was a surprisingly large hall and would have looked rather like the interior of a Norman cathedral. The one at Chester, for example, was about 73 metres (240 feet) long; its central nave, bounded by tall columns supporting a vaulted roof, was 12 metres (40 feet) wide and flanked by two aisles each of 6 metres (20 feet). If each man had stood shoulder to shoulder, it would just have been possible to squeeze the entire legion into it. Whether this was ever done we do not know.

In the centre of the far long wall of the basilica and directly facing the main gate was the most sacred place in the fortress, the 'sacellum' or chapel. This housed the standard of the legion, the 'aquila', an image of an eagle perched with outspread wings on the top of a pole. It was made of gold and in its talons it clutched a bundle of golden darts that represented the thunderbolts of Jupiter. The aquila represented 'the spirit of the legion' and aroused feelings of intense loyalty and an almost religious respect. To lose it in battle was the worst possible disgrace and misfortune; it rarely happened. The soldier who looked after the aquila and carried it in battle (see the picture on p.75) was called the 'aquilifer' (eagle-bearer). He was always a soldier of the first cohort.

On either side of the sacellum were the rooms where the clerks kept the payrolls and attended to all the paperwork that was needed to run a large unit. Close by and usually underground was the legion's strong-room, in which pay and savings were kept under lock and key.

The praetorium was situated by the side of or just behind the principia. It was a fine house in the style of an Italian 'domus urbāna' and it provided the legatus and his family with those comforts which they would regard as necessary for a civilised life: central heating, a garden and a private suite of baths. These luxuries were provided for the legatus, partly because he was the commander and partly because he was a member of the highest social class and would therefore expect it. But there was probably another reason, namely to demonstrate the attractions of Roman civilisation to local civilian leaders, who were no doubt entertained in the praetorium from time to time. However, whether this display of wealth made them any happier about the taxes which they had to pay to the Romans is another question.

The valetudinarium or hospital contained many small wards for the sick and injured. There was also a large reception hall and a small operating theatre equipped with running water.

Model of stone granaries

The horrea were skilfully designed to keep grain dry and cool for long periods. In the first century A.D., like many other buildings in the fortress, they were built mainly of wood, but from the second century stone was the regular material. A granary was a long and narrow building; the roof had wide overhanging eaves to carry the rain-water away from the walls; and to prevent damp rising from the ground the floor was supported on small piers or low walls which allowed air to circulate freely underneath. There were several of these granaries in a fortress, often arranged side by side in pairs, and they could contain stocks of grain sufficient at least for one year and possibly two.

Clearly the barrack blocks, housing 5,000–6,000 men, occupied the largest area. They too were long and narrow; and they were divided into pairs of rooms, each pair providing accommodation for an eight-man section (contubernium). Along the front of the block ran a colonnaded verandah. Each section cooked for itself on a hearth in the front living-room, which was slightly the smaller of the two rooms, and slept in the larger room at the back. Each block housed a century (80 men). At the end of the block a larger suite of rooms was provided for the centurion, who may have shared it with his optio. The blocks themselves were arranged in pairs facing each other across an alley-way, as in the diagram below.

contubernia

The bathhouse was regarded as an important part of military hygiene; every fortress and many smaller forts had one. Like the civilian baths, it consisted of a tepidarium, caldarium and frigidarium and served as a social club. Sometimes the military baths were outside the fortress, by a nearby stream or river, sometimes inside.

One other building, always outside, should be mentioned: the amphitheatre. It had the same shape and layout as the civilian amphitheatre and could seat the whole legion. It was used for ceremonial parades, weapon training and displays of tactics, as well as for occasional gladiatorial shows.

Not surprisingly, civilians also tended to gather round military bases. At first they were traders who set up little bars to sell appetising food and drink to supplement the plain rations served in the barracks. Naturally, too, these bars gave soldiers opportunities to meet the local girls. Legally soldiers were not allowed to marry, but the army tolerated unofficial unions. While the father lived in barracks his family grew up just outside; and his sons when they were eighteen or nineteen often followed his profession and enlisted. Many such settlements (vīcī) developed gradually into towns. A few became large, self-governing cities, such as Eboracum (York). Thus the military fortress, which had begun as a means of holding down newly conquered territory, ended by playing an important part in the development of civilian town life.

Words and phrases checklist

adeō – so much, so greatly
aditus, aditūs – entrance
adventus, adventūs – arrival
anteā – before
appāreō, appārēre, appāruī – appear
ardeō, ardēre, arsī – burn, be on fire
certāmen, certāminis – struggle, fight
comes, comitis – comrade, companion
decet – it is proper
   mē decet – I ought
fax, facis – torch
gaudeō, gaudēre – be pleased, rejoice
ignārus, ignāra, ignārum – not knowing, unaware
imperō, imperāre, imperāvī – order, command
incendō, incendere, incendī, incēnsus – burn, set fire to
īnsidiae, īnsidiārum – trap, ambush
iocus, iocī – joke
iussum, iussī – order
manus, manūs – band (of men)
noceō, nocēre, nocuī – hurt
occurrō, occurrere, occurrī – meet
ōsculum, ōsculī – kiss
praeceps, *gen.* praecipitis – headlong
praemium, praemiī – prize, reward
proximus, proxima, proximum – nearest
quālis, quāle – what sort of
silentium, silentiī – silence
sub – under, beneath
tacitus, tacita, tacitum – silent
taedet – it is tiring
   mē taedet – I am tired, I am bored
tantus, tanta, tantum – so great, such a great

imperium

post mortem Cogidubnī, Salvius rēgnum eius occupāvit. pecūniam
ā Britannīs extorquēre statim coepit. Salvium adiuvābat Belimicus,
prīnceps Canticōrum.

   prope aulam habitābat agricola Britannicus, quī Salviō
pecūniam trādere nōluit. Salvius igitur mīlitibus imperāvit ut
casam agricolae dīriperent. centuriōnem mīlitibus praefēcit.

mīlitēs, gladiīs hastīsque
armātī, casam agricolae
oppugnāvērunt.

agricola, gladiō centuriōnis
vulnerātus, exanimātus
dēcidit.

servī, clāmōribus territī,
fūgērunt.

fīlius agricolae, fūste armātus,
frūstrā restitit.

Belimicus, spē praemiī
adductus, mīlitēs Rōmānōs
adiuvābat et incitābat.

mīlitēs casam intrāvērunt et
arcam, pecūniā complētam,
extulērunt.

deinde mīlitēs fēminās, catēnīs vīnctās, abdūxērunt.

postrēmō mīlitēs casam incendērunt. flammae, ventō auctae, casam celeriter cōnsūmpsērunt.

pāstōrēs, quī prope casam habitābant, immōtī stābant, spectāculō attonitī.

casam vīdērunt, flammīs cōnsūmptam.

fīlium agricolae vīdērunt, hastā graviter vulnerātum.

agricolam ipsum vīdērunt, gladiō centuriōnis interfectum.

tandem abiērunt, timōre īrāque commōtī, Belimicum Rōmānōsque vituperantēs.

testāmentum

ego, Tiberius Claudius Cogidubnus, rēx magnus Britannōrum, morbō gravī afflīctus, hoc testāmentum fēcī.
ego Titum Flāvium Domitiānum, optimum Imperātōrum, hērēdem meum faciō. mandō T. Flāviō Domitiānō rēgnum meum cīvēsque Rēgnēnsēs. iubeō cīvēs Rēgnēnsēs lēgibus pārēre et vītam 5 quiētam agere. nam prīncipēs Rēgnēnsium mē saepe vexāvērunt. aliī, spē praedae adductī, inter sē pugnāvērunt; aliī, īnsāniā affectī, sēditiōnem contrā Rōmānōs facere temptāvērunt. nunc tamen eōs omnēs oportet discordiam huius modī dēpōnere.
    dō lēgō Cn. Iūliō Agricolae statuam meam, ā fabrō Britannicō 10 factam. sīc Agricola mē per tōtam vītam in memoriā habēre potest.
    dō lēgō C. Salviō Līberālī, fidēlissimō amīcōrum meōrum, duōs tripodas argenteōs. Salvius vir summae prūdentiae est.
    dō lēgō L. Marciō Memorī vīllam meam prope Aquās Sūlis sitam. L. Marcius Memor, ubi aeger ad thermās vēnī, ut auxilium ā deā 15 Sūle peterem, benignē mē excēpit.
    dō lēgō Dumnorigī, prīncipī Rēgnēnsium, quem sīcut fīlium dīlēxī, mīlle aureōs aulamque meam. sī forte Dumnorix mortuus est, haec C. Salviō Līberālī lēgō.
    dō lēgō Belimicō, prīncipī Canticōrum, quīngentōs aureōs et 20 nāvem celerrimam. Belimicus enim mē ab ursā ōlim servāvit, quae per aulam meam saeviēbat.
    mandō C. Salviō Līberālī cūram fūneris meī. volō Salvium corpus meum sepelīre. volō eum mēcum sepelīre gemmās meās, paterās aureās, omnia arma quae ad bellum vēnātiōnemque comparāvī. 25
    mandō C. Salviō Līberālī hoc testāmentum, manū meā scrīptum ānulōque meō signātum. dolus malus ab hōc testāmentō abestō!

lēgibus: lēx *law*	mīlle *a thousand*
praedae: praeda *booty, plunder*	celerrimam: celer *quick, fast*
adductī: addūcere *lead on, encourage*	corpus *body*
affectī: afficere *affect*	sepelīre *bury*
discordiam: discordia *strife*	dolus . . . abestō! *may . . .*
in memoriā habēre *keep in mind, remember*	*trickery keep away!*
benignē *kindly*	malus *evil, bad*
excēpit: excipere *receive*	

When you have read each section, answer the questions that follow it.

in aulā Salviī

I

Salvius, cum dē morte Cogidubnī audīvisset, ē castrīs discessit. per prōvinciam iter fēcit ad aulam quam ē testāmentō accēperat. ibi novem diēs manēbat ut rēs Cogidubnī administrāret. decimō diē, iterum profectus, pecūniās opēsque ā Britannīs extorquēre incēpit. plūrimī prīncipēs, avāritiā et metū corruptī, Salvium adiuvābant. 5

Belimicus, prīnceps Canticōrum, spē praemiī adductus, Salviō summum auxilium dedit. Britannōs omnia bona trādere coēgit. aliī, quī potentiam Salviī timēbant, Belimicō statim cessērunt; aliī, quī eī resistēbant, poenās gravēs dedērunt.

Belimicus autem, quamquam prō hōc auxiliō multa praemia 1 honōrēsque ā Salviō accēpit, haudquāquam contentus erat. rēx enim Rēgnēnsium esse cupiēbat. hāc spē adductus, cum paucīs prīncipibus coniūrāre coepit. quī tamen, Belimicō diffīsī, rem Salviō rettulērunt.

Salvius, audāciā Belimicī incēnsus, eum interficere cōnstituit. amīcōs igitur, quibus maximē cōnfīdēbat, ad sē vocāvit; eōs in aulam ingressōs rogāvit utrum vim an venēnum adhibēret. amīcī, ut favōrem Salviī conciliārent, multa et varia cōnsilia prōposuērunt.

tandem ūnus ex amīcīs, vir callidissimus,

'venēnum', inquit, 'Belimicō, hostī īnfestō, aptissimum est.'

'sed quō modō tālem rem efficere possumus?' inquit Salvius. 'nam Belimicus, vir magnae prūdentiae, nēminī cōnfidit.'

'hunc homunculum dēcipere nōbīs facile est', inquit ille. 'venēnum cibō mixtum multōs virōs callidiōrēs quam Belimicum iam fefellit. ipse sciō venēnum perītē dare.'

'euge!' inquit Salvius, cōnsiliō amīcī dēlectātus. 'facillimum est mihi illum ad cēnam sūmptuōsam invītāre. mē oportet epistulam blandam eī mittere. verbīs enim mollibus ac blandīs resistere nōn potest.'

Salvius igitur Belimicum ad aulam sine morā invītāvit. quī, 30 epistulā mendācī dēceptus neque ūllam fraudem suspicātus, ad aulam nōnā hōrā vēnit.

decimō: decimus *tenth*
profectus *having set out*
avāritiā: avāritia *greed*
metū: metus *fear*
prō *for, in return for*
bona *goods*
haudquāquam *not at all*
rettulērunt: referre *tell, report*
audāciā: audācia *boldness, audacity*
incēnsus *inflamed, angered*
utrum . . . an *whether . . . or*
favōrem: favor *favour*
conciliārent: conciliāre *win, gain*

īnfestō: īnfestus *dangerous*
aptissimum: aptus *suitable*
mixtum: miscēre *mix*
fefellit: fallere *deceive*
sūmptuōsam: sūmptuōsus *expensive, lavish*
blandam: blandus *flattering*
mollibus: mollis *soft*
morā: mora *delay*
neque *and not*
ūllam: ūllus *any*
fraudem: fraus *trick*
nōnā: nōnus *ninth*

1 Where does Salvius travel to when he hears of Cogidubnus' death?
2 How long does Salvius stay there? Why?
3 What does Salvius do next? How does Belimicus help him?
4 Why does Belimicus stop helping Salvius and start plotting?
5 How does Salvius find out about Belimicus' plot?
6 What decision does Salvius take when he hears of Belimicus' treachery? What question does he put to his friends?
7 Which suggestion does Salvius accept? What are the advantages of this method?
8 How does he lure Belimicus into his trap?

II

Belimicum aulam intrantem Salvius benignē excēpit et in triclīnium
addūxit. ibi sōlī sūmptuōsē atque hilarē cēnābant. Belimicus,
Salvium rīdentem cōnspicātus vīnōque solūtus, audācter dīcere
coepit.

'mī Salvī, multa et magna beneficia ā mē accēpistī. postquam
effūgērunt Quīntus et Dumnorix, ego sōlus tē adiūvī; multōs
continuōs diēs eōs persecūtus Dumnorigem occīdī; multa falsa
Agricolae dīxī ut Cogidubnum perfidiae damnārem; post mortem
eius, Britannōs pecūniam bonaque sua trādere coēgī. prō hīs tantīs
beneficiīs praemium meritum rogō.'

Salvius, ubi haec audīvit, arrogantiā Belimicī incēnsus, īram
tamen cēlāvit et cōmiter respondit.

'praemium meritum iam tibi parāvī. sed cūr nihil cōnsūmis, mī
amīce? volō tē garum exquīsitissimum gustāre quod ex Hispāniā
importāvī. puer! fer mihi et Belimicō illud garum!'

136

cum servus garum ambōbus dedisset, Salvius ad hospitem versus,

'dīc mihi, Belimice', inquit, 'quid prō hīs tantīs beneficiīs repetis?'

'iam ex testāmentō Cogidubnī', respondit ille, 'quīngentōs aureōs accēpī. id haudquāquam satis est. rēgnum ipsum repetō.'   20

quod cum audīvisset, Salvius 'ego', inquit, 'nōn Cogidubnus, aureōs tibi dedī. cūr haud satis est?'

'quid dīcis?' exclāmāvit Belimicus. 'hoc nōn intellegō.'

'illud testāmentum', respondit Salvius, 'est falsum. nōn Cogidubnus sed ego scrīpsī.'   25

addūxit: addūcere *lead*
sūmptuōsē *lavishly*
atque *and*
hilarē *in high spirits, merrily*
vīnō . . . solūtus *relaxed by the wine*
persecūtus *having pursued*
damnārem: damnāre *condemn*
meritum: meritus *well-deserved*
Hispāniā: Hispānia *Spain*
repetis: repetere *claim*
haud *not*

1 How is Belimicus received and treated when he comes to the palace?
2 What makes Salvius angry (line 11)? Why do you think he hides his anger?
3 What does Belimicus think Salvius means by a 'praemium meritum' (line 13)? What does Salvius really mean?
4 During the meal, Belimicus changes his tactics: instead of continuing with his plot, he asks Salvius directly for the kingship. What has encouraged him to do this?
5 What has Belimicus already received? How? What does he now learn about the will?

About the language

1   Study the following sentences:

iuvenis, **gladiō** armātus, ad castra contendit.
The young man, armed with a sword, hurried to the camp.

Britannī, **tantā iniūriā** incēnsī, sēditiōnem fēcērunt.
The Britons, angered by such great injustice, revolted.

mīles, **vulnere** impedītus, tandem cessit.
The soldier, hindered by his wound, gave in at last.

senex, **multīs cūrīs** vexātus, dormīre nōn poterat.
The old man, troubled by many cares, was unable to sleep.

cīvēs, **clāmōribus** excitātī, ē lectīs surrēxērunt.
The citizens, awakened by the shouts, rose from their beds.

The words in heavy print are in the *ablative* case.

2   Compare the nominative singular with the ablative singular and ablative plural in the first, second and third declensions:

	nominative singular	*ablative singular*	*ablative plural*
1st declension	puella	puellā	puellīs
2nd declension	servus	servō	servīs
	puer	puerō	puerīs
	templum	templō	templīs
3rd declension	mercātor	mercātōre	mercātōribus
	leō	leōne	leōnibus
	cīvis	cīve	cīvibus
	rēx	rēge	rēgibus
	urbs	urbe	urbibus
	nōmen	nōmine	nōminibus

3 Further examples:

1 Salvius, audāciā Belimicī attonitus, nihil dīxit.
2 mercātor, fūstibus verberātus, in fossā exanimātus iacēbat.
3 mīlitēs, vallō dēfēnsī, barbarīs diū resistēbant.
4 uxor mea ānulum, gemmīs ōrnātum, ēmit.
5 hospitēs, arte ancillae dēlectātī, plausērunt.

Belimicus rēx

Belimicus, cum haec audīvisset, adeō attonitus erat ut nihil respondēre posset. Salvius autem haec addidit rīdēns,
'mī amīce, cūr tam attonitus es? tū et Cogidubnus semper inimīcī erātis. num quicquam ab illō spērāvistī? nōs autem in amīcitiā sumus. tibi multum dēbeō, ut dīxistī. itaque rēgem tē creāre in 5 animō habeō. sed rēgnum quod tibi dēstinō multō maius est quam Cogidubnī. heus! puer! plūs garī!'
servus, cui Salvius hoc imperāvit, statim exiit. brevī regressus, garum venēnō mixtum intulit atque in Belimicī pateram effūdit. tam laetus erat ille, ubi verba Salviī audīvit, ut garum cōnsūmeret, 10 ignārus perīculī mortis.
'quantum est hoc rēgnum quod mihi prōmīsistī? ubi gentium est?' rogāvit Belimicus.
Salvius cachinnāns 'multō maius est', inquit, 'quam imperium Rōmānum.' 15
Belimicus hīs verbīs perturbātus,
'nimium bibistī, mī amīce', inquit. 'nūllum rēgnum nōvī maius quam imperium Rōmānum.'
'rēgnum est, quō omnēs tandem abeunt', respondit Salvius. 'rēgnum est, unde nēmō redīre potest. Belimice, tē rēgem creō 2• mortuōrum.'
Belimicus, metū mortis pallidus, surrēxit. haerēbat lingua in gutture; tintinnābant aurēs; ventrem, quī iam graviter dolēbat, prēnsāvit. metū īrāque commōtus exclāmāvit,
'tū mihi nocēre nōn audēs, quod omnia scelera tua Agricolae 2• dēnūntiāre possum.'
'mē dēnūntiāre nōn potes, Belimice, quod nunc tibi imminet mors. nunc tibi abeundum est in rēgnum tuum. avē atque valē, mī Belimice.'
Belimicus, venēnō excruciātus, pugiōnem tamen in Salvium coniēcit, spē ultiōnis adductus. deinde magnum gemitum dedit et humī dēcidit mortuus. Salvius, pugiōne leviter vulnerātus, servō

imperāvit ut medicum arcesseret. aliī servī corpus Belimicī ē
triclīniō extractum quam celerrimē cremāvērunt. sīc Belimicus
arrogantiae poenās dedit; sīc Salvius cēterīs prīncipibus persuāsit ut 35
in fidē manērent.

spērāvistī: spērāre *hope, expect*
creāre *make, create*
dēstinō: dēstināre *intend*
effūdit: effundere *pour out*
ubi gentium? *where in the world?*
perturbātus: perturbāre *disturb, alarm*
lingua *tongue*
gutture: guttur *throat*
tintinnābant: tintinnāre *ring*
ventrem: venter *stomach*

graviter dolēbat: graviter dolēre
  be extremely painful
scelera: scelus *crime*
dēnūntiāre *denounce, reveal*
imminet: imminēre *hang over*
tibi abeundum est *you must go away*
avē atque valē *hail and farewell*
excruciātus: excruciāre *torture, torment*
leviter *slightly*
cremāvērunt: cremāre *cremate*

About the language

1 Study the following examples:

lēgātus sermōnem cum Quīntō **duās hōrās** habēbat.
The commander talked with Quintus for two hours.

quattuor diēs fugitīvus in silvā latēbat.
For four days, the runaway lay hidden in the wood.

In each of these sentences, the words in heavy print indicate *how long* something went on; for this, Latin uses the *accusative* case.

2 Now study the following:

tertiā hōrā nūntiī advēnērunt.
At the third hour, the messengers arrived.

quīntō diē Agricola pugnāre cōnstituit.
On the fifth day, Agricola decided to fight.

In these sentences, the words in heavy print indicate *when* something happened; for this, Latin uses the *ablative* case.

3 Further examples:

1 hospitēs trēs hōrās cēnābant.
2 quārtō diē revēnit rēx.
3 Agricola prōvinciam septem annōs administrāvit.
4 secundā hōrā lībertus Memorem excitāre temptāvit.
5 mediā nocte hostēs castra nostra oppugnāvērunt.
6 sex diēs nāvigābāmus; septimō diē ad portum advēnimus.

Practising the language

1 Study the form and meaning of the following adjectives and nouns, and give the meaning of the untranslated words:

avārus	greedy, miserly	avāritia	greed
amīcus	friendly	amīcitia	friendship
superbus	proud	superbia	
trīstis		trīstitia	
perītus		perītia	skill, experience
sapiēns		sapientia	
prūdēns		prūdentia	sense
perfidus	treacherous, untrustworthy	perfidia	
ēlegāns	elegant, tasteful	ēlegantia	
benevolēns	kind	benevolentia	

Give the meaning of the following nouns:

laetitia, audācia, arrogantia, īnsānia, potentia

2 Complete each of the sentences below with one of the following groups of words and then translate. Use each group of words once only.

ut nēmō centuriōnem audīret
ut Belimicum interficeret
ut ad castra redīrent
quō modō Cogidubnus periisset
cum tabernam intrāvissent

1 Salvius cibum venēnō mixtum parāvit . . . .
2 Quīntus nesciēbat . . . .
3 cīvēs, ..., vīnum poposcērunt.
4 tantus erat clāmor . . . .
5 Agricola mīlitibus imperāvit . . . .

3 Complete each sentence with the most suitable word from the list below, and then translate.

audāciā, vīnō, gladiō, īrā, catēnīs

1 nūntius, ... graviter vulnerātus, effugere nōn poterat.
2 Salvius, ... eius attonitus, diū tacēbat.
3 captīvī, ... vīnctī, in longīs ōrdinibus stābant.
4 dominus, ... commōtus, omnēs / servōs carnificibus trādidit.
5 hospitēs, ... solūtī, clāmāre et iocōs facere coepērunt.

About the language

1 From Stage 1 onwards, you have met phrases of the following kind:

ad fundum   to the farm
ex ātriō   out of the hall
per viās   through the streets
cum amīcīs   with friends

The words in heavy print are *prepositions*. A preposition is normally used with a noun in the accusative or ablative case.

2 The prepositions 'ad', 'per' and 'prope' are used with the *accusative*:

ad **rēgem**   to the king
per **flammās**   through the flames
prope **sellam**   near the chair

Other prepositions used with the accusative are 'ante', 'circum', 'contrā', 'extrā', 'inter', 'post' and 'trāns'.

3 The prepositions 'ā', 'ab', 'cum', 'ē' and 'ex' are used with the *ablative*:

> ab **amphitheātrō**   from the amphitheatre
> ex **oppidō**   out of the town
> cum **hospitibus**   with the guests

Other prepositions used with the ablative are 'dē', 'prō' and 'sine'.

4 Notice how the preposition 'in' is used:

cīvēs **in forum** cucurrērunt.	The citizens ran into the forum.
mercātōrēs **in forō** negōtium agēbant.	The merchants were doing business in the forum.
ancilla centuriōnem **in tabernam** dūxit.	The slave-girl led the centurion into the inn.
canis **in tabernā** dormiēbat.	The dog was sleeping in the inn.

'in' meaning '*into*' is used with the accusative.
'in' meaning '*in*' is used with the ablative.

5 Further examples:

1 duo amīcī ad urbem iter faciēbant.
2 prope templum deae erat fōns sacer.
3 prīncipēs dē morte Belimicī sermōnem habēbant.
4 prō aulā stābant quattuor custōdēs.
5 mīlitēs in castrīs labōrābant.
6 Agricola in castra contendit.
7 centuriō sine mīlitibus revēnit.
8 gubernātor nāvem circum saxum dīrēxit.

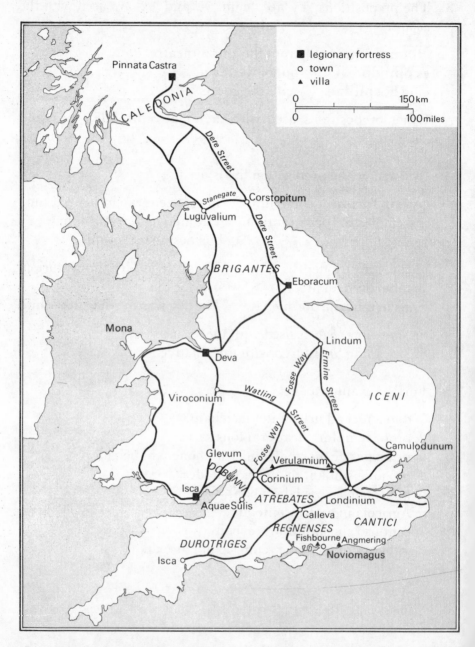

Britain in the first century A.D.

Interpreting the evidence : our knowledge of Roman Britain

Our knowledge of the Roman occupation of Britain is based on three types of evidence:
(1) *literary* evidence: what the Romans wrote about Britain;
(2) *archaeological* evidence: what archaeologists have discovered during excavations, including:
(3) *inscriptional* evidence: inscriptions in Latin (and sometimes Greek) from tombstones, altars, public buildings and monuments, and from private objects such as writing-tablets, defixiones etc.

All of this material has to be interpreted before we can begin to understand it. The writings have to be translated and the exact meanings of technical terms have to be found; discoveries made on an archaeological site have to be noted down and different periods identified so that remains can be dated; inscriptions have to be deciphered, translated and, where possible, dated. It is a long and complicated process, in which one type of evidence can often help us to understand another type. To see how it works in practice, we shall examine examples from each type of evidence.

Literary evidence

There are two well-known Latin writings about Roman Britain. One is Julius Caesar's account in which he describes his brief reconnaissance mission to the Kent coast in 55 B.C. and his return in greater force the following year when he stormed the fortress of a British king before withdrawing again. The other is Tacitus' account of the life of his father-in-law, Agricola. More than half of this is devoted to Agricola's governorship of Britain, including such exploits as the circumnavigation of Britain and the defeat of the Scots in the great battle of Mons Graupius.

Both pieces of writing are to some extent biased. Caesar wrote his account in order to justify his actions to the Senate in Rome and place himself in a favourable light; Tacitus was anxious to preserve the memory of his father-in-law and to praise his success as governor.

In chapter 21 of his biography, Tacitus tells us that under Agricola an extensive programme of romanisation was carried out, including the building of 'fora' or town centres in some of the larger and well-established settlements in the south-east of Britain. This was confirmed by the discovery, during an excavation, of fragments of an inscription which was designed to stand over the entrance to the new forum at Verulamium (St Albans). It mentions the name of Agricola in connection with the building of the forum. (A reproduction of the inscription appears on p. 108.)

Tacitus also tells us of Roman plans to improve the education of the British:

> 'Agricola arranged for the sons of British chiefs to receive a broad education. He made it clear that he preferred the natural abilities of the British to the skill and training of the Gauls. As a result, instead of hating the language of the Romans, they became very keen to learn it.'

This may sound as if Tacitus is exaggerating. However, we know from inscriptions that Salvius, who was a distinguished lawyer, was sent to Britain at about this time, and one of his tasks may have been to help the British bring their laws into line with Roman law. If this was so, there may be a link between Salvius' presence in Britain and Tacitus' statement that the British were eager to learn Latin; they may have wished not only to have conversations with the occupying forces, but also to understand the complexities of Roman law.

Archaeological evidence

The task of an archaeologist is to uncover and to help us understand the remains of the past. To do this he or she must first decide on a suitable site to excavate. Some sites are already well-known but have not been completely excavated; sometimes sites are found by accident. A workman digging a drain across a field in 1962 hit fragments of a mosaic floor and this chance discovery led to the excavation of the palace at Fishbourne. Building and road works can often uncover evidence of a site. In such cases archaeologists may have a very limited time in which to excavate before the bulldozers move in and destroy the evidence for ever.

Once the site has been located, the archaeologist has to plan and carry out a careful excavation of the area. This means uncovering the foundations of buildings, mosaic floors and other large structures, and carefully sifting the soil for pieces of pottery, items of jewellery, coins and other small objects. However, the purpose of an excavation is not simply to find precious objects but to discover as much as possible about the people who used the buildings, what their life was like, when they lived there and even perhaps what happened to them. In order to do this an archaeologist must be trained, rather like a detective, to observe every small detail and to piece together all the evidence that is found.

As the earth is removed from a site, the archaeologist will watch for two things: the existence and position of any wall foundations, and the way in which the various levels or layers of earth change colour and texture as the trenches are dug deeper. If one wall is built directly on top of another, it is reasonable to assume that the lower wall is from an earlier building.

Roman coins can usually be accurately dated because they have the emperors' heads and names stamped on them. If a coin of Nero is found in a layer, then the date of the layer can be no earlier than A.D. 54 since Nero was not emperor until then. If no coins of later emperors are found in the layer, then it is reasonable to assume that the layer dates from Nero's reign (A.D. 54 to 68) or from the short period afterwards during which coins of Nero's reign continued to circulate.

Fairly accurate dates are also obtainable from a study of the styles and patterns of pottery found on a site. Large quantities have survived, as pottery is a durable material which does not rot, and broken pieces (sherds) are found in very large numbers on many sites. All kinds of pottery were used throughout the Roman world and the presence on a British site of pottery which has come from Italy or Gaul shows that the owner was wealthy enough to pay for imported material. In ways such as this the archaeologist can begin to assemble information about the people who occupied the site.

Layers of ash, charred pottery and other burnt objects will indicate a destruction by fire; a mass of broken rubble may suggest that a building was demolished, perhaps to make way for a larger, better one. Many sites in Britain show a gradual development from a simple timber-framed farmhouse building, which was replaced by a larger stone house, to a grander, multi-roomed mansion with baths, mosaic pavements and colonnades.

By such painstaking processes archaeologists have been able to reconstruct a remarkably detailed picture of the Roman occupation of Britain. The fact that most of the Romano-British villas were sited in the south-east, whereas the military fortresses were established in the north and west, suggests that Britain at this period was largely peaceful and prosperous in the south-east but still troubled by the threat of hostile tribes in the north-west. Traces of a vast network of Roman roads have been found, showing just how numerous and effective communications must have been. Parts of many Romano-British towns have been excavated, revealing how advanced urban life was. It is not uncommon to find the remains of an extensive forum, carefully laid out grids of streets, the foundations of many large buildings including temples with altars and inscriptions, sometimes a theatre and an amphitheatre, and substantial city walls.

The excavation of military sites, such as forts, marching camps and legionary fortresses, has shown how important the army was in maintaining peace and protection for Roman Britain. It has also shown very clearly the movements of the legions around the country and added considerably to our knowledge of the Roman army.

A.D.
1900–1960 Modern topsoil

1100–1900 Mediaeval and later plough soil

270–400 Abandoned site robbed for building stone
270 Palace destroyed by fire
110–270 Later development. Reflooring dated by coin of 197
75 Palace. Stone walls and mosaic floors on rubble foundations. Local and imported stone

44–70 Civil development

43–4 Military period. Post hole, Claudian coins, pottery, fragments of military equipment

Diagram showing layers of evidence for occupation at Fishbourne

Inscriptional evidence

Some important evidence about the Roman occupation of Britain comes from inscriptions, particularly on the tombstones of soldiers. Here is the inscription on the tombstone of a soldier who was buried at Chester.

D M

L LICINIUS L F

TER   VALENS

ARE VETERAN

LEG XX VV AN VL

H S E

At first sight, this looks difficult to decipher. The task, however, is made easier by the fact that most of these inscriptions follow a standard pattern. The items are usually arranged in the following order:

(1) The dedication at the top of the stone – D M – abbreviation for 'Dīs Mānibus', the spirits of the departed.
(2) The praenomen. This is first of a citizen's three names and is usually abbreviated to a single letter, as here – L for 'Lūcius'.
(3) The nomen. Always given in full, as here – 'Licinius'.
(4) The father's name. It is usually only the father's praenomen that is given, and this can be recognised in abbreviated form by the single letter which comes before an F representing 'fīlius'. The son often had the same praenomen as his father, as here – L F for 'Lūciī fīlius'.
(5) Tribe. Roman soldiers were Roman citizens and were therefore enrolled in one of the thirty-five Roman tribes. The name of the tribe is abbreviated, as here – TER for 'Teretīna'.
(6) The cognomen. This is the last of the three names, usually placed after the father's name and the Roman tribe in which the soldier was enrolled. It is always given in full, as here – 'Valēns'. Three names were a mark of Roman citizenship and therefore an important indication of status.

(7) Birthplace. This can usually be identified as a town in the Roman empire, thus ARE for 'Arelātē' (modern Arles in the south of France).

(8) Rank and legion. They are usually both abbreviated – VETERAN for 'veterānus'; LEG XX VV for 'legiōnis XX Valeriae Victrīcis'.

(9) Age. This is represented by AN or ANN for 'annōrum', followed by a number. This number is in most cases rounded off to a multiple of 5. Sometimes VIX ('vīxit' = lived) is placed before AN.

(10) Length of service (not included in the inscription above). This is represented by STIP followed by a number, e.g. STIP X for 'stipendia X' (ten years' service).

(11) The final statement. This is abbreviated, and usually takes the form of H S E for 'hīc situs est' (is buried here) or H F C for 'hērēs faciendum cūrāvit' (his heir had this stone set up).

The Chester inscription can therefore be interpreted as follows:

D(IS) M(ANIBUS)
L(UCIUS) LICINIUS L(UCII) F(ILIUS)
TER(ETINA) VALENS
ARE(LATE) VETERAN(US)
LEG(IONIS) XX V(ALERIAE) V(ICTRICIS) AN(NORUM)
V L
H(IC) S(ITUS) E(ST)

This stone is dedicated to the spirits of the departed. Lucius Licinius Valens, son of Lucius, of the Teretine tribe, from Arelate, veteran of the Twentieth Legion Valeria Victrix, aged 45, is buried here.

Here is the inscription on another soldier's tombstone, also found at Chester.

D M
CÆCILIVS·AVIT
VS·EMER·AVG
OPTIO LEG XX
VV STP·XV·VIX.
AN.XXXIIII
H   F   C

Try to find out from it the following information:

1 The soldier's name   4 His age at death
2 His rank   5 The length of his service
3 His legion

In the same way, find as much information as you can from the following inscription:

8   17   32

(41)

Words and phrases checklist

ac – and

arrogantia, arrogantiae – cheek, arrogance

atque – and

beneficium, beneficiī – act of kindness, favour

cōnstituō, cōnstituere, cōnstituī, cōnstitūtus – decide

corpus, corporis – body

dīligō, dīligere, dīlēxī, dīlēctus – be fond of

doleō, dolēre, doluī – hurt, be in pain

gemitus, gemitūs – groan

hērēs, hērēdis – heir

īra, īrae – anger

lingua, linguae – tongue

malus, mala, malum – evil, bad

mandō, mandāre, mandāvī, mandātus – entrust, hand over

metus, metūs – fear

mīlle – a thousand

mīlia – thousands

multō – much

occīdō, occīdere, occīdī, occīsus – kill

opēs, opum – money, wealth

pallidus, pallida, pallidum – pale

praeficiō, praeficere, praefēcī, praefectus – put in charge

quicquam (*also spelt* quidquam) – anything

sīc – thus, in this way

solvō, solvere, solvī, solūtus – loosen, untie

spēs, speī – hope

suspicātus, suspicāta, suspicātum – having suspected

testāmentum, testāmentī – will

ut – as

ventus, ventī – wind

ūnus – one	vīgintī – twenty
duo – two	trīgintā – thirty
trēs – three	quadrāgintā – forty
quattuor – four	quīnquāgintā – fifty
quīnque – five	sexāgintā – sixty
sex – six	septuāgintā – seventy
septem – seven	octōgintā – eighty
octō – eight	nōnāgintā – ninety
novem – nine	centum – a hundred
decem – ten	ducentī – two hundred